30-Minute Meatless Cookbook

30-Minute
Meatless
Cookbook

Delicious Vegetarian
Recipes for Busy People

PAIGE RHODES

ROCKRIDGE
PRESS

**To Chris and Renee, my parents and biggest cheerleaders.
Your support in all my endeavors is appreciated more than you know.**

Interior and Cover Designer: Amanda Kirk
Art Producer: Samantha Ulban
Editor: Owen Holmes
Production Editor: Ashley Polikoff
Production Manager: David Zapanta

Photography © 2022 Elysa Weitala, Cover; © Andrew Purcell, pp. ii, 16, 60; © Hélène Dujardin, p. viii, 104; © Emulsion Studio, pp. 38, 84; © Darren Muir, 104; © Nat & Cody Gantz, p. 53. All other images used under license Shutterstock. Food Styling by Victoria Woollard, Cover.
Cover image: Vegetable Lo Mein with Tofu, page 134

Paperback ISBN: 978-1-638-78210-0
Ebook ISBN: 978-1-638-78705-1
R0

CONTENTS

INTRODUCTION

Let me guess—you picked up this book after feeling lost with your redundant weeknight meals. Perhaps you're a lifelong vegetarian who wants to bring it back to basics or a newbie who doesn't know where to start. Maybe you're setting out on a temporary journey of eliminating meat for health reasons, or you're trying to support your newly vegetarian son or daughter. Whatever brings you here, welcome. Hats off to you for taking the initiative to expand your dinner horizons and seeking out inspiration when you needed it most.

Thanks to social media and a variety of cooking shows on television, more people are learning how enjoyable the cooking process can be, and switching up your diet seems more attainable than ever. Everyone wants delicious food, but unfortunately time is getting harder and harder to come by. And although there are now abundant recipes available for plant-based foods, that doesn't always mean it's convenient. That's where this book comes in. I want to show you that you can be creative and put together impressive vegetarian dinner spreads all within 30 minutes or fewer. (Yes, it's possible!) Look, we're all busy people just trying to fuel our bodies the best way we know how. Choosing to eat vegetarian may throw an extra obstacle in the plot, but this book will show you that it doesn't have to be a challenge.

My name is Paige, by the way. I'm a cookbook author, food blogger, recipe developer, and lifelong carnivore turned veggie curious over the last couple of years. You read that right—I'm not a full-fledged vegetarian. In my opinion, this gives me a well-rounded view of cooking and makes me extra picky as to what makes a great hearty vegetarian meal. After all, you want a meal that would please both meat eaters and vegetarians alike.

As a mother who also runs her own business, it's always important to me that food be accessible and quick without sacrificing flavor and nutrition. I take it very seriously that you're trusting me with the task of curating meals for you and your crew, and for that, I'm so grateful.

Going meatless looks a lot different today than it did even five years ago. No matter the dish you're trying to make, there's very likely a meat-free substitute that will look almost identical to its original counterpart. Whether it's bacon, chicken nuggets, or even tuna, you can waltz right into any grocery store and be greeted with a multitude of meat-free options. It can be overwhelming, to be honest. Even restaurants have so many more vegetarian dishes on their menus now. Gone are the days that you had to order something "without the chicken."

Let's be real, we're not all professional chefs who can conceptualize a meal in seconds. In the chapters that follow, you'll find recipes for reimagined favorites like Spaghetti with Mushroom Bolognese (page 114) and Cauliflower Mac and Cheese (page 138), along with showstopping dishes like Hot Honey Corn Ribs (page 128) and Sweet and Salty Chopped Broccoli Salad (page 52). You'll also discover the building blocks of creating your vegetarian masterpieces, along with the tools you need to get dinner on the table in a flash. There may even be a few secrets for recipe variations and saving even more time preparing a meal. I hope this book invigorates your love for cooking or, at the very least, makes it a pleasant process that you no longer dread. Deciding to go vegetarian is a huge step, one that you should be applauded for, should you choose to take it. Whether you're fully committed or just cutting back on meat, sit back, relax, and let me help you on your journey with tried-and-true vegetarian meals.

CHAPTER 1

Meatless Made Simple

Before introducing the delicious recipes, we've got some house-keeping to do. In the first chapter of this book, I'll share the fundamentals of getting a meatless meal on the table in 30 minutes or fewer, what you should include on your plate for well-rounded nutrition, pantry must-haves, and more. The information and tips you'll read here will help you better understand the recipes and become a more intuitive vegetarian cook overall.

Quick & Easy Vegetarian Meals

Over the last decade, rising concerns over the environmental impact of livestock raising, transport, and processing have prompted more people to turn to vegetarian eating. Couple that with the often inhumane conditions and treatment of the animals, and suddenly health and wellness aren't the only reasons that folks are opting to go meatless.

Nutrition is always at the forefront, however, and it can be challenging finding the time to make that a priority. It's not as simple as walking into the grocery store and picking out something from the deli counter (unless you want all sides, that is). The fact is, being a vegetarian takes some forethought, but that doesn't mean you have to spend half your day planning out meals. I get that life is hectic. This book offers you a plan—meals that are balanced, tasty, and can be prepared in 30 minutes or fewer. Whether you're a seasoned veggie alum who is looking for some new weeknight inspiration or a curious newbie who has no idea where to start, I offer a few key principles to help you in the kitchen.

Efficient cooking techniques. Although I love to braise and roast vegetables, I often rely on sautéing or steaming when I'm trying to get the job done quickly. These methods are both quick and easy without sacrificing time or flavor.

Embrace raw vegetables. I know what you're thinking, but hear me out. Raw doesn't have to mean salads only. In addition to a handful of tasty sammies and luxe sauce recipes, the Cucumber-Herb Gazpacho (page 82) and Tropical Turmeric Smoothie (page 32) are two of my favorite recipes that require no cooking.

Bold flavors. Give me anything spicy, pickled, or full of herbs. The truth is, the more flavor you add to the dish, the less you have to do to achieve that well-rounded taste you're looking for.

Smaller knife cuts. It might seem simple, but the smaller you slice and dice, the quicker your food will cook. Thinking about making a vegetarian meatloaf but are short on time? Go for the Cranberry-Jalapeño Swedish "Meatballs" (page 132) instead.

Quick-cooking grains. Grains are a big part of vegetarian cooking, but some can take a long time to fully cook. Although risotto is delicious, it's hard to get that done in fewer than 30 minutes. Try using a short-cut pasta like orzo, or opt for quinoa, farro, or instant rice to build your bowls and sides.

What This Book Means by "Meatless"

As with most things, vegetarianism isn't black and white. If someone considers themselves a pescatarian, that means they still enjoy fish from time to time. An ovo-vegetarian still eats eggs, and a lacto-vegetarian consumes dairy products. The recipes you'll find in this book are considered lacto-ovo, a mix of the two. So you'll still see dairy and eggs, but no meat or seafood. You'll also occasionally be given a substitution tip to make a recipe vegan, which means there are no animal products or by-products whatsoever, like cheese, milk, eggs, etc. Even if you call yourself a flexitarian (like me) and occasionally eat meat, you'll still benefit greatly from this book.

Building a Balanced Meal in 30 Minutes

There is a common misconception that a vegetarian lifestyle is inherently healthy. I know plenty of vegetarians who often eat a plate of French fries and peanut butter cups for dinner. While the recipes in this book are designed to be quick and easy, they're good for you as well. It's always important to aim for a nutritious diet with balanced macronutrients.

POWERFUL PROTEINS

Extra-firm tofu: Tofu is one of the most well-rounded and nutrient-dense ingredients you can add to your vegetarian arsenal. It contains all the essential amino acids your body needs and is one of the best sources of plant protein. Although there's some chatter about too much soy causing harm, tofu is widely considered safe for most people to include in their diet regularly.

Lentils: Lentils are made up of more than 25 percent protein, making them an excellent meat alternative. They're also a great source of iron, a mineral that is sometimes lacking in vegetarian diets, and high in fiber, which we all need for optimal gut health. Bonus: They're very affordable and serve as the perfect base for salads, bowls, and soups.

Eggs: Raise your hand if the media has confused you about the healthiness of eggs in the past. The truth is, eggs are one of the most nutritious foods we can eat. They contain a percentage of almost every vitamin and mineral our bodies require, including calcium, iron, potassium, zinc, manganese, vitamin E, and folate. Not to mention the whopping 6 grams of protein per egg. Talk about getting a lot of bang for your buck.

Oats: Speaking of protein, one serving of oats also boasts a satiating 6 grams. Add to the fact that it's filled with good fiber and other nutrients, and it's a breakfast powerhouse. I love to stir egg whites into my oats in the morning for even more of a protein boost.

Beans: If I could list each legume individually, I would. In this book, you'll find mostly chickpeas and black beans, but white beans and kidney beans also make an appearance. Pro tip: Beans are an incomplete protein source on their own, but pairing them with a grain like rice means you're getting a complete source of protein, much like chicken.

COMPLEX CARBS

100 percent whole-wheat pasta: One hundred percent whole-wheat pasta includes all three layers of the wheat kernel: the bran, the germ, and the endosperm. Because it is less processed, whole-wheat pasta contains more natural fiber and minerals such as magnesium, iron, and zinc than white pasta. This keeps you full longer and makes sure those blood sugar levels are in check.

Quinoa: Not only is quinoa an amazing complex carbohydrate, but it also has a good amount of protein and even a small amount of omega-3 fatty acids to boot. Complex carbs are made of longer, more complex chains of sugar molecules and take longer to digest than simple carbs do. That means sustained energy versus a quick burst.

Sweet potatoes: If you're a runner, sweet potatoes will be your best friend when fueling up before your trek because they'll give you that boost you need without the stomachache. White potatoes and corn are also complex carbs, but not quite as nutritious. Fun fact: The deeper the hue of the sweet potato, the higher it is in antioxidants.

Brown rice: As with whole-wheat pasta, brown rice is whole-grain rice with the hull, the bran layer, and the cereal germ intact, whereas they are removed in white rice. The result is a nutty flavor that makes brown rice the perfect hearty base for all your favorite Buddha bowls.

Carrots: Do you ever wake up in the middle of the night with terrible hunger pangs? Try eating a serving of nonstarchy complex carbs like carrots as a bedtime snack. Carrots are so versatile that they're perfect for breakfast, lunch, and dessert.

FILLING FATS

Avocado: I know I don't need to convince you to join the avocado fan club, but hear me out. You'll find avocado throughout this book because it's so versatile and chock-full of heart-healthy monounsaturated fats, which are what you're going for.

Nuts: Depending on which one you're eating, nuts are made of up to 80 percent fat, which is why your nut butter usually needs a good stir before using. Whether you're making a sauce with peanut butter or using walnuts in faux ground meat, nuts are essential for a plant-based diet, so long as you're not allergic.

Full-fat coconut milk: Thanks to its thick consistency and rich, creamy texture, coconut milk is a great alternative to dairy in soups and sauces. Its fat comes from medium-chain triglycerides, or MCTs, that are said to help keep you feeling full.

Olive oil: Since vegetarians can't rely on fish for omega fats, olive oil is the best source with both omega-3 and omega-6 fatty acids. It's not only my go-to for cooking with but also for making dressings and drizzling on top of finished dishes.

Cheese: In moderation, cheese and other dairy products help nonvegans fill in the nutritional gaps that eliminating meat can create. In addition to their fat content, dairy products will give you a healthy dose of calcium and vitamins D and B_{12} that you may lack on a vegetarian diet.

VITAMINS AND SUPPLEMENTS

Vitamin B_{12}: Meat is a huge source of B_{12}, which is why most vegetarians need to supplement to make sure they're getting plenty of this vitamin through foods like cheese, milk, and yogurt. Vegans can try eating more root vegetables, mushrooms, and nutritional yeast.

Iron: Iron is found in two forms: heme and non-heme. Heme iron is only found in animal products, whereas non-heme iron comes from plants. To avoid anemia, eat plenty of cruciferous veggies, and try cooking in a cast-iron skillet!

Vitamin D: Vitamin D deficiency is a problem with vegetarians as well as meat eaters. Although it's hard to get enough of the fat-soluble vitamin without supplementation, fortified plant milk or juice and sun exposure are a great place to start.

Zinc: Thankfully, whole grains, tofu, legumes, nuts, and seeds are great sources of zinc, all of which you'll find plenty of in this book. Bonus absorption happens when you soak dried beans overnight before using, so try that out instead of using canned beans.

● Vegetarian on the Fly

Now that you know the building blocks of a nutritious and well-balanced vegetarian meal, it's time to put it all into practice. Even with these amazing recipes, there will still be nights when you need to throw a bowl together and go. I highly recommend prepping a bunch of staples at the beginning of the week so you can pull different items to make your meal. For optimal mealtime success, pick two carbs, two proteins, and two sauces or dressings from the list to prep for the week. Then, when you're ready to eat, make your desired veggies and toppings right before.

To build the perfect bowl, start by choosing a complex carb to serve as your base, then move on to the veggies. I like to pick at least two veggies to start, and they could be greens like kale or spinach, frozen vegetables, or leftovers. Next comes the protein. I typically go for one, but sometimes I'll pair an egg with something like beans for a little boost. I'll usually go for two fats like chopped nuts with a dressing, etc. Finally, we have the seasonings and toppings. I'll opt for a couple of these as well for as much flavor as possible. Seeds, herbs, and anything pickled are always my go-to, but you do you!

1. Choose a complex carb.

- Quinoa
- Rice
- Millet
- Sweet potato
- 100 percent whole-wheat pasta
- Sprouted toast

2. Choose some veggies.

- Salad greens like kale, baby spinach, arugula, or spring mix
- Roasted sweet potatoes
- Broccoli
- Cauliflower
- Sliced bell peppers
- Spiralized carrots or zucchini

3. Choose a protein.

- Regular or smoked tofu, cubed
- Marinated and baked tempeh
- Beans and lentils
- Quinoa
- Hemp seeds
- Eggs
- Homemade veggie burgers

4. Choose one or two fats.

- Lemon-Tahini Sauce (page 149)
- Cashew-Basil Pesto (page 143)
- Avocado
- Hemp seeds
- Dressing
- Chopped nuts

5. Add toppings or seasonings.

- Chopped fresh herbs
- Toasted pumpkin seeds
- Pickled Red Onions (page 144)
- Crispy Garlic Chickpeas (page 148)
- Everything bagel seasoning
- Red pepper flakes

Shopping Shortcuts

I promise that no one will think you're a hero if you make a point to chop all your onions by hand. Getting a little help with prep work is an important part of putting dinner on the table in a timely fashion, and these are my favorite ways to do it without sacrificing flavor.

Canned beans: Soaking and slow-cooking beans is great every once in a while if you have some extra time on the weekend. However, 9 times out of 10, I'm whipping out my can opener to use beans in a recipe, and so should you.

Spice blends: Trader Joe's is the best place to buy inexpensive spices, but spice blends in general will be your best friend. Everything bagel seasoning is a favorite, with Italian seasoning and taco seasoning close behind.

Frozen vegetables: I can't tell you how many frozen vegetables I have in my freezer right now. Vegetables are always frozen at their peak ripeness, so they're often even more nutritious than their fresh counterparts. Frozen soup starters with carrots, onions, and celery are always extremely helpful.

Boxed vegetable broth: Vegetable and mushroom broth are invaluable when making vegetarian sauces and soups. Sure, you could use water instead, but broth adds so much depth of flavor. You can also buy vegetable bouillon base so you can make broth whenever you want in a pinch.

Precooked rice: Rarely do I ever make rice from scratch. Using precooked grains is one of my favorite ways to save time. Trader Joe's has a great selection of frozen cooked rice and vacuum-packed lentils that I love to use, but you can find them at most grocery stores.

Prechopped garlic: Nothing quite beats fresh garlic, but I know that many people refuse to chop it themselves. You can go for the jars of prechopped garlic in the produce section, but if you can find frozen cubes of garlic, they're almost as good as fresh.

Spiralized veggies: Remember when we all bought spiralizers, never to use them? If you didn't, you're lucky because now you can buy spiralized vegetables fresh in the produce section or in frozen steamable bags as well.

⬤ Your Secret Pantry Arsenal

One of the ways you can keep things easy, healthy, and tasty in your kitchen is through curating a selective, strategic pantry. You probably have all the basic spices and condiments already, but these are the standout players that I would never be without.

Sriracha: I'd be lying if I said I didn't have a hot sauce for every mood, but when all else fails, sriracha is the one I reach for most often to spice up any dish.

Full-fat coconut milk: In everything from smoothies to curries, coconut milk is the MVP of plant-based milk, in my opinion. Make sure to buy canned coconut milk for optimal creaminess, not the carton variety.

Canned tomatoes: Fire-roasted, diced, crushed, and whole tomatoes are always fully stocked in my pantry. Whether you're making a marinara sauce or hearty chili, if you have tomatoes on hand, you can come up with a delicious dinner in no time.

Garam masala: This spice blend contains both savory and warming spices like cardamom, nutmeg, cloves, cumin, and peppercorns. The flavor is unmatched, and the boldness means you don't need to add a lot of other spices to your dish.

Vinegar: It's so hard to pick just one, but apple cider vinegar, red wine vinegar, white wine vinegar, rice vinegar, and balsamic vinegar are my favorites and add the perfect amount of acidity to a dish when you don't have fresh citrus available.

Nutritional yeast: Even though I'm not vegan, I love the cheesy, nutty flavor of nutritional yeast. I use it any time I want to make a vegan cashew sauce. It's amazing blended into a dressing, and any that's left over can be sprinkled on popcorn or used to top a power bowl.

Soy sauce: It's embarrassing the amount of soy sauce I go through. You can find it at any grocery store, and I use it almost every day. I love marinating tofu with it, adding it to dressings, and finishing off ramen with it.

Quick Veggie Prep

One of the major qualms people have with cooking, especially when so many veggies are involved, is the sheer amount of prep that goes into it. Every recipe in this book is designed to take 30 minutes or fewer, so at least you know that no matter what, you're not going to spend any more time than that in the kitchen. That being said, there are ways you can make even quicker work of prep.

In almost every recipe, you'll be dicing a vegetable, be it onions, carrots, or celery. I like to gather up all my ingredients in front of me and get them ready by cutting off the ends and removing any rough outer layers or peeling if necessary. Then everything is ready to go so I can run my knife through each item quickly.

Shredding veggies like carrots or cabbage can seem like a drag (and scary for your knuckles), but it doesn't have to be. If you have a food processor, you can use the shredding attachment to get it done in seconds, or you can buy preshredded veggies.

When a recipe calls for an ingredient, typically garlic or ginger, to be minced, that indicates a really fine dice. Instead of using your big knife to do this, try rubbing it back and forth on your Microplane grater, and you'll get the finest mince possible.

Since legumes are a vital protein source for vegetarians, you'll be doing a lot of draining and rinsing canned beans for the recipes. I like to use a fine-mesh strainer to drain the beans and then rinse them until they're no longer foamy to ensure that the excess starches have been removed.

Bell peppers and spicy peppers need to be seeded and sliced in many recipes throughout the book. An easy way to do this is to stand the pepper up on its bottom and slice it downward vertically around the stem in planks. Then you can discard the stem and seeds and proceed with slicing or dicing.

● Surprisingly Nonvegetarian Foods

Veteran vegetarians probably know all the unlikely animal products that are hidden in some foods, but newbies may be surprised to learn what to look out for. Most issues arise with processed or prepackaged foods, but it's good to prepare for what labels you need to scour.

Parmesan and other imported cheeses: These sometimes contain rennet, which is an enzyme from a cow's stomach used to separate milk in the cheesemaking process. When in doubt, ask a knowledgeable cheesemonger for cheeses made with vegetarian-friendly alternatives such as vegetable rennet and microbial rennet. (You can also safely buy fresh cheeses that don't contain rennet at all: think cream cheese and paneer.)

Caesar dressing: We will make our dressing for the Chickpea Caesar Salad (page 57) from scratch, but almost all store-bought Caesar dressings contain anchovies.

Marshmallows: Anything that contains gelatin, like marshmallows, Jell-O, candy corn, and even gummy vitamins, is a no-go for vegetarians. Gelatin is made from the skin, hooves, and bones of animals, so it is definitely noncompliant.

Refried beans: It seems like a trick, but a majority of refried beans are made with lard, especially the ones from authentic Latin brands. When in doubt, just check the label, but don't worry—there is almost always a vegetarian option close by.

Processed sugar: This was a recent discovery for me, and I was so shocked at how hard it was to find true vegetarian sugar. Most types of processed sugar are refined using an outdated product known as bone char. I'll spare you the details, but it's used to remove impurities from raw sugar. The bone char doesn't show up in the final product at the store, but it may be a problem for strict vegetarians. Raw cane sugar is usually a safe bet.

Convenient Plant-Based Cooking Tools

Almost as important as the ingredients are the tools used to cook the meal. Time is priceless, and the right kitchen equipment can make or break the mealtime process. If you fill your cabinets with a few fundamental utensils, gadgets, and pans, then there's nothing else standing in the way of your weeknight cooking success.

ESSENTIAL EQUIPMENT

Sharp knife. I'm sure you already have a kitchen knife, but a good-quality knife will go a long way in prepping all those veggies. Knife sharpeners are fairly cheap and will keep all your blades in line for years.

High-speed blender: A good blender can do the job of several tools. You'll need one for the Tropical Turmeric Smoothie (page 32) and the Cucumber-Herb Gazpacho (page 82).

Cutting board: Your landlord won't appreciate you chopping your vegetables on the counter. Grab a few (especially if you have meat eaters in the house) to avoid cross-contamination and so you can prep more than one ingredient at a time.

Sheet pans: Pick up a set with a few different sizes and you can have Carrot Cake Breakfast Cookies (page 34) baking while you're roasting veggies.

Silicone baking mat: These are perfect for easy sheet-pan cleanup without wasting aluminum foil or parchment paper. You'll be thankful that you took the extra step when you have fewer dishes to wash.

Whisk: You wouldn't think this would be a time-saver, but when you're trying to get lumps out of a sauce or emulsify a dressing with a fork, you'll think differently.

Stainless steel or glass mixing bowls with lids: These are great for prepping veggies, marinades, and sauces ahead to save valuable minutes later on. I love to make a marinade for tofu in a bowl and then let the tofu sit in the mixture with the lid on in the refrigerator until I'm ready to cook.

Herb scissors: If you hate chopping herbs with a passion, a pair of herb scissors is a fun way to get the job done.

GADGETS FOR PEOPLE WHO HATE PREP

These tools aren't necessary to have in your kitchen, but they can make prep work a lot easier and help you get dinner on the table even sooner.

 Food processor: Although a blender can handle a lot, some jobs are better suited for a food processor. If dicing vegetables isn't your jam, a food processor or an onion chopper will help you until your knife skills improve.

 **Small handheld mandoline:** In the time it would take you to cut two thin slices of cucumber with a knife, you could have the whole cucumber sliced with a mandoline. Just make sure to use the handguard because they're very sharp, and you'll be well on your way to making French Onion Rigatoni (page 124).

 Microplane grater: This is one of the most versatile kitchen gadgets that I use for zesting citrus, grating hard cheese, mincing garlic, or grinding nutmeg.

Vegetable peeler: Some people find it easier to use a paring knife, and some prefer to use a vegetable peeler to remove those pesky skins. If you're not confident with a knife, then a peeler will be an invaluable tool.

● Healthy Your Way

On top of the 65 amazing vegetarian meals in the book, I've included 10 staple recipes that will help take your dishes over the top. Chapter 7 includes homemade condiments, sauces, dressings, toppings, and dips. All these staples can easily be purchased at the grocery store if you like, but if you want to go the homemade route, they're here for you. For example, if you decide to make VLT Sandwiches (page 88), you'll see an asterisk next to Vegetarian Bacon (page 142) in the ingredient list, sending you to the recipe for homemade Vegetarian Bacon in chapter 7. There will also be a shortcut tip marked with an asterisk for the store-bought version.

Shortcut: Vegetarian bacon comes in many forms at the grocery store. Some are found in the freezer section, while others are located in the refrigerated section with other plant-based goods. I love to use Lightlife Tempeh Smoky Bacon, which has a great texture and flavor.

One of the reasons I love using tempeh bacon as opposed to some of the other meat alternatives is that the ingredients are much simpler and more wholesome. Tempeh is made from fermented soybeans, giving it a dense texture and nutty flavor. It can be sliced and panfried to use in myriad vegetarian dishes. Try to steer clear of vegan bacon that has modified cornstarch, wheat gluten, hydrolyzed corn protein, vegetable glycerin, or artificial colors or flavors added. When looking for store-bought sauces, keep an eye out for unnecessary gums or emulsifiers, and opt for olive and avocado oils instead of soybean or canola oils. I'm all about a quick fix here and there but certainly not at the expense of flavor and, most important, health!

About the Recipes

The best thing about this book is that the recipes take 30 minutes or fewer to prepare, start to finish, with many of them taking only 15 minutes. Besides that, each recipe features different labels, tips, and callouts to help guide you along the way.

Labels to help navigate. At the top of each recipe, you'll find labels that indicate various dietary and time alerts. The **Superfast** label is reserved for recipes that take 15 minutes or less to prepare from start to finish, including prep. We can all use that on busy nights, right? The **Gluten-Free** and **Dairy-Free** labels appear when applicable, and you'll see the **Vegan** label when a recipe is completely plant based with no substitutions needed. Always check ingredient packaging for gluten-free labeling (in order to ensure foods, especially oats, were processed in a completely gluten-free facility).

Tips that make it even easier. Everyone can use a tip or two sometimes, and you'll spot them on at least half of the recipes in the book. If you see a recipe with a **Smart Shopping** tip, you'll learn how to buy a specific ingredient in season, where to look, or what to look for on a label. The **Make It Faster** tips allow you to prepare a recipe quicker by using a certain technique, omitting a step, or preparing something ahead. Aside from those, you will also find tips about varying the recipe in terms of ingredients or flavors, working with a particular ingredient, or using leftovers creatively.

Optional homemade staples. The very last chapter in the book contains recipes for my **Homemade Staples**. These recipes consist of homemade condiments, sauces, dressings, toppings, and dips. If a homemade staple is called for in a recipe in another chapter, you'll see an annotation to refer to it for further instruction. The homemade staples are some of my favorites, and you'll be adding them to all your meals before long!

This book was made for adventurous cooks and newbies alike. Whether you're a food-show fanatic who loves to try new veggie-loaded meals or you're just starting out on your vegetarian cooking journey, you'll find a multitude of recipes that will be with you forever. Now, on to the good stuff!

Mixed Berry
Cornmeal Muffins,
page 22

CHAPTER 2

Breakfasts

Jalapeño Frittata

● GLUTEN-FREE

Serves 4 to 6 / **Prep time:** 5 minutes / **Cook time:** 25 minutes

Frittatas are an elegant way to serve eggs, and they're far easier to make than most people imagine, especially if you have a cast-iron or oven-safe skillet. Cooked in the oven, there's no need to worry about flipping your frittata onto a plate or delicately folding it like an omelet. Don't let the idea of using 12 jalapeños scare you off. When they're baked with the eggs and cheese, the heat is mellow and pleasant.

8 large eggs

12 jalapeños, seeded and cut into rounds

1½ cups grated aged Cheddar cheese, divided

2 tablespoons extra-virgin olive oil

1 onion, sliced

1 cup grape tomatoes

1 tablespoon chopped fresh basil leaves

1. Preheat the oven to 375°F.

2. Break the eggs into a large mixing bowl, and using a whisk, beat well.

3. Add the jalapeños and 1 cup of cheese. Whisk until combined.

4. In a 10-inch cast-iron or oven-safe skillet, heat the oil over medium heat.

5. When the oil is hot, add the onion and fry for 3 to 4 minutes, or until soft.

6. Add the tomatoes and stir for 1 minute.

7. Toss in the basil and stir for a few seconds.

8. Pour the egg mixture into the skillet, and cook undisturbed for 4 minutes while the bottom sets. Remove from the heat.

9. Transfer the skillet to the oven and bake for 15 minutes, or until the eggs have set in the center, which you can test using a cake tester or a toothpick.

10. As soon as the frittata has set, remove from the oven, leaving the oven on. Top with the remaining ½ cup of cheese.

11. Turn on the broiler and carefully move the oven rack up to the top position.

12. Place the skillet under the broiler for a couple minutes, or until the cheese is bubbling and the top has nicely browned. Remove from the oven.

13. Run a rubber spatula around the edges of the skillet to loosen the sides, then slide the frittata onto a large serving plate.

14. Cut the frittata into wedges and serve hot.

Smart Shopping: Sliced pickled jalapeños in a jar and bagged pre-grated Cheddar cheese can be purchased to save time slicing and grating. Use 1 teaspoon of dried basil in place of the fresh basil.

Per Serving: Calories: 406; Total fat: 31g; Carbohydrates: 8g; Fiber: 2g; Protein: 25g; Sodium: 408mg

Pumpkin-Spiced Pancakes

Serves 4 / **Prep time:** 15 minutes / **Cook time:** 15 minutes

The second autumn rolls around, you're going to be craving these pancakes. The fragrant warming spices of cinnamon, cloves, and allspice will make your house smell like a pie factory—cue the salivating. The pancakes are light and fluffy, even though they are made with whole-wheat flour, so no one will suspect that they are healthy as well. Thankfully, canned pumpkin is sold year-round so you can enjoy these pancakes whenever you like.

1¼ cups whole-wheat flour

1 tablespoon raw cane sugar

2 teaspoons baking powder

1 teaspoon ground cinnamon

¼ teaspoon ground cloves

⅛ teaspoon ground allspice

¾ teaspoon sea salt

1⅓ cups whole milk

¾ cup canned pumpkin puree

4 large eggs

4 tablespoons (½ stick) unsalted butter, melted

1 teaspoon vanilla extract

¼ cup canola oil or clarified butter

¾ cup warm maple syrup

1. Sift the flour, sugar, baking powder, cinnamon, cloves, allspice, and salt into a large bowl. Mix to blend.

2. In a medium bowl, whisk together the milk, pumpkin puree, eggs, butter, and vanilla until well blended.

3. To make the batter, add the pumpkin mixture to the dry ingredients and whisk until just smooth.

4. Heat a large nonstick sauté pan or skillet over medium heat. Brush with the oil.

5. Pour the batter into the skillet in ⅓-cup measures. Cook for about 2 minutes, or until bubbles form on the surface of the pancakes and the bottoms have browned.

6. Flip the pancakes and cook the other side for about 2 minutes. Transfer to a plate and cover loosely with aluminum foil to keep warm. Repeat with any remaining batter to make 8 pancakes.

7. Serve the pancakes with the maple syrup.

Tip: I like to add caramelized apple slices and toasted pepitas to garnish these beautiful pancakes. Any kind of fruit compote or fresh fruit is a wonderful complement to this dish.

Per Serving (2 pancakes): Calories: 668; Total fat: 34g; Carbohydrates: 79g; Fiber: 6g; Protein: 14g; Sodium: 362 mg

Mixed Berry
Cornmeal Muffins

Makes 12 muffins / Prep time: 5 minutes / **Cook time:** 20 minutes

Making muffins at home is not as challenging and time-consuming as you might think, and you'll have some leftovers to enjoy for breakfast or as a snack for a few days. Very little sugar is added to these moist and cakey muffins because they are bursting with the naturally sweet goodness of antioxidant-rich fresh berries. Dark chocolate chips are optional, but they do add texture and depth to the flavor. Feel free to use any kind of milk you prefer (dairy, coconut, and almond are all good options).

Oil or nonstick cooking spray, for greasing the muffin tin

1½ cups all-purpose flour

¾ cup yellow cornmeal

⅓ cup raw cane sugar

4 teaspoons baking powder

¼ teaspoon sea salt

¾ cup fresh blueberries

½ cup fresh raspberries or blackberries

⅓ cup dark chocolate chips (optional)

1 large egg

1 cup milk

¼ cup extra-virgin olive oil

1½ teaspoons vanilla extract

1. Preheat the oven to 400°F. Grease the cups of a 12-cup muffin tin with oil.

2. In a large bowl, whisk together the flour, cornmeal, sugar, baking powder, and salt.

3. Stir in the blueberries, raspberries, and chocolate chips (if using). Make a well in the center of the mixture.

4. In a small bowl, lightly beat the egg.

5. Add the milk, olive oil, and vanilla to the egg. Whisk until well combined.

6. Pour the egg mixture into the well in the flour mixture and stir gently until just combined.

7. Spoon the mixture evenly into the prepared muffin cups.

8. Transfer the muffin tin to the oven and bake for 15 to 20 minutes, or until a cake tester or toothpick inserted into the middle of each muffin comes out clean. Remove from the oven. Let sit for a few minutes, then transfer to a wire rack to cool slightly. Serve warm or at room temperature.

Tip: For moist, light, and airy muffins, take care not to overmix the batter. Stir the wet ingredients into the dry ingredients until everything is just combined.

Per Serving (1 muffin): Calories: 149; Total fat: 6g; Carbohydrates: 23g; Fiber: 1g; Protein: 3g; Sodium: 70mg

Egg-in-a-Hole Avocado Toast

● **DAIRY-FREE** ● **SUPERFAST**

Serves 4 / **Prep time:** 5 minutes / **Cook time:** 10 minutes

My absolute favorite breakfast as a kid was egg-in-a-hole, or egg-in-a-basket, as some call it. I didn't have the pleasure of adding avocado back then, but it's essential for me now. If you have kiddos at home, they'll enjoy assembling this breakfast as much as eating it. If you're making only one or two servings, this dish can easily be made in a toaster oven.

**4 hearty whole-grain
bread slices**

4 large eggs

**2 ripe avocados,
pitted and peeled**

¼ teaspoon sea salt

**1 tablespoon everything bagel
seasoning**

½ cup sliced cherry tomatoes

**2 tablespoons minced scallions,
both white and green parts**

1. Preheat the oven to 400°F. Line a rimmed sheet pan with unbleached parchment paper.

2. Using a 3-inch biscuit cutter (or the top of a 3-inch-wide glass), make a hole in the center of each bread slice.

3. Evenly space the slices on the prepared sheet pan and crack 1 egg into each hole. Lay a cutout bread round next to each slice.

4. Transfer the sheet pan to the oven and bake for 4 minutes. Flip the bread rounds only and bake for 4 more minutes, or until the egg whites have set but the yolks are still runny. Remove from the oven.

5. While the toast bakes, in a small bowl, mash together the avocados and salt.

6. Spread one-quarter of the mashed avocados onto each slice of toast around the egg.

7. Sprinkle each slice with the everything bagel seasoning, then top with the tomatoes and scallions.

8. Serve each avocado toast with a cutout bread round to dip in the yolk.

Smart Shopping: Read the label on the everything bagel seasoning, and omit the sea salt listed in the recipe if it's already included.

Per Serving: Calories: 317; Total fat: 21g; Carbohydrates: 24g; Fiber: 9g; Protein: 12g; Sodium: 303mg

Savory Zucchini and Oatmeal Breakfast Bowls

● **GLUTEN-FREE** ● **SUPERFAST**

Serves 4 / **Prep time:** 5 minutes / **Cook time:** 10 minutes

If you've yet to cross over to the savory side of oats, you are in for a pleasant surprise. This dish has an enjoyable creaminess and a hint of garlic that really ties it all together. It's a great way to sneak some zucchini into your family's diets, as well as healthy fats and protein. One bite of these, and you'll be wondering why sweet oats were the standard all this time.

4 cups water

2 cups certified gluten-free rolled oats

2 zucchini, grated

1 teaspoon garlic powder

½ teaspoon sea salt

¼ teaspoon freshly ground black pepper

4 large eggs

1 cup shredded Parmesan cheese

2 ripe avocados, pitted, peeled, and sliced

¼ cup chopped fresh parsley

1 tablespoon hemp seeds (optional)

1. In a saucepan, bring the water to a boil over high heat.

2. Stir in the oats, zucchini, garlic powder, salt, and pepper. Cover the saucepan and reduce the heat to low. Simmer for 5 minutes. Remove from the heat.

3. While the oats are cooking, prepare the eggs to your preference—scrambled, fried, and soft-boiled are all good choices. Set aside.

4. Stir the cheese into the cooked oats, cover, and let sit for 1 minute.

5. Divide the oats among 4 bowls. Top each bowl with 1 egg, a few slices of avocado, a sprinkle of parsley, and a pinch of hemp seeds (if using).

Tip: If you're a fan of heat, top with a drizzle of sriracha or other hot sauce before serving.

Per Serving: Calories: 414; Total Fat: 22g; Carbohydrates: 45g; Fiber: 10g; Protein: 14g; Sodium: 625mg

Sheet Pan Egg and Cheese Sandwiches

Serves 4 / **Prep time:** 10 minutes / **Cook time:** 10 minutes

This is one of my absolute favorite ways to power my morning, whether I'm hitting the road in a hurry or fueling after a workout. You can buy egg rings at most kitchen stores—or use round metal cookie cutters in a pinch. If those methods don't work for you, feel free to cook the scrambled eggs on the stovetop before assembling the sandwiches.

Nonstick cooking spray, for coating the egg rings

4 large eggs

2 tablespoons milk of choice

Pinch salt

Pinch freshly ground black pepper

4 tablespoons (½ stick) unsalted butter

4 English muffins, split

4 Cheddar cheese slices

1 cup chopped spinach

4 tomato slices

4 teaspoons sriracha

1. Line a rimmed sheet pan with parchment paper and put it in the oven. Preheat the oven to 350°F. Coat 4 (3½-inch) egg rings with cooking spray.

2. In a bowl, whisk together the eggs and milk. Season with the salt and pepper.

3. Spread the butter on the English muffin halves.

4. Carefully remove the sheet pan from the oven. Place the greased egg rings on it.

5. Divide the egg mixture among the egg rings.

6. Place the English muffins, buttered-sides up, on the sheet pan.

7. Return the sheet pan to the oven and bake for 8 minutes.

8. Place the cheese slices on the English muffin tops and bake for 2 more minutes, or until the cheese has melted. Remove from the oven.

9. Carefully remove the eggs from the egg rings and place them on the English muffin bottoms.

10. Top each egg with ¼ cup of spinach and a tomato slice.

11. Drizzle each sandwich with 1 teaspoon of sriracha.

12. Cover the sandwiches with the English muffin tops.

Tip: **Prepare the sandwiches as directed through step 9, then wrap tightly with plastic wrap and store in a zip-top bag in the freezer for up to 1 month. Defrost in the refrigerator the night before you plan to eat them. Remove the sandwich from the plastic wrap and wrap it in a paper towel. Microwave for 1 minute, flip, and microwave for 30 more seconds, or until warmed through. Add fresh spinach and tomato and serve.**

Per Serving: Calories: 426; Total fat: 27g; Carbohydrates: 29g; Fiber: 2g; Protein: 18g; Sodium: 708mg

Quick Chilaquiles

● **GLUTEN-FREE**

Serves 4 / **Prep time:** 10 minutes / **Cook time:** 20 minutes

Chilaquiles are the ultimate breakfast food, in my opinion. They're delicious, filling, and incredibly easy to make. Even though this is a quick recipe as is, if you want to make it even more speedy, you can use your favorite store-bought tortilla chips instead of making your own. I recommend buying the thickest chips you can find to avoid sogginess, but doing this will save you about 15 minutes. You can't beat that.

16 (6-inch) corn tortillas

¼ cup avocado oil

1 tablespoon unsalted butter

4 large eggs

1 (10-ounce) can gluten-free red enchilada sauce

¼ cup crumbled Cotija cheese

2 tablespoons chopped fresh cilantro

2 radishes, thinly sliced

2 tablespoons Pickled Red Onions (page 144)*

Cilantro-Lime Crema (page 150), for serving (optional)

1. Stack a few tortillas at a time, and cut each tortilla into 8 wedges.

2. In a large skillet, heat the oil over medium-high heat until just shimmering. (You can test the temperature of the oil by seeing if a small piece of tortilla placed in the oil sizzles.) Line a plate with paper towels.

3. When the oil is hot, add one-quarter of the tortilla wedges at a time and cook, flipping once, for 2 to 3 minutes total, or until lightly browned and crisp. Repeat until all the tortillas have been fried. Transfer to the prepared plate to drain.

4. Discard the excess cooking oil, and using a paper towel, carefully wipe out the skillet. Melt the butter in the skillet over medium heat.

5. Crack the eggs directly into the skillet and cook to your desired doneness, ideally for about 3 minutes so the yolks are still runny. Transfer to a plate.

6. Increase the heat to medium-high. In the same skillet, heat the enchilada sauce for about 3 minutes, or until just warmed through. Remove from the heat.

7. Add the tortilla chips to the skillet and toss to fully coat with the sauce.

8. Top with the eggs, cheese, cilantro, radishes, pickled red onions, and crema (if using). Serve immediately.

● ***Shortcut: If you like, you can use thinly sliced raw red onions or scallions instead.**

Per Serving: Calories: 478; Total fat: 26g; Carbohydrates: 50g; Fiber: 6g; Protein: 14g; Sodium: 127mg

Tropical Turmeric Smoothie

● **GLUTEN-FREE** ● **SUPERFAST** ● **VEGAN**

Serves 2 / **Prep time:** 5 minutes

Smoothies are my go-to whenever I don't want to think too much about my breakfast. This one is perfect in the winter months when you may have a lingering cold you need to care for or if you simply wish you were on the beach. Sometimes I swap out the mango for pineapple, add a little fresh ginger for spice, or throw in a carrot or frozen cauliflower for added nutrients. If using frozen mango and papaya chunks, feel free to omit the ice.

1 banana, peeled and sliced

1 cup full-fat coconut milk

1 cup fresh mango chunks

1 cup fresh papaya chunks

2 mandarin oranges, peeled and separated

1 (1-inch) piece fresh turmeric root, peeled and sliced

1 cup ice

Put the banana, coconut milk, mango, papaya, oranges, turmeric, and ice in a high-powered blender. Blend until smooth. Serve immediately.

● **Make It Faster:** I love to prep a bunch of fruit at one time and make smoothie packs to freeze that I can grab and throw in the blender whenever I like. I'll even freeze my coconut milk in ice cube trays to add to the bags. If you do this, omit the ice.

Per Serving: Calories: 444; Total fat: 25g; Carbohydrates: 58g; Fiber: 9g; Protein: 5g; Sodium: 26mg

Cinnamon-Peach Ricotta Toast

● SUPERFAST
Serves 4 / Prep time: 10 minutes

I'm a big believer that sometimes the simplest dishes are the best. With this toast, each flavor has its moment to shine, and they all go so perfectly with one another. If you like a hint of heat, you could top with a sprinkle of red pepper flakes or swap out the honey for hot honey for a subtle kick. I like to add a bit more cinnamon and flaky sea salt on top to balance the sweetness.

1 cup whole-milk ricotta cheese

¼ cup honey

½ teaspoon ground cinnamon

Pinch salt

8 sourdough bread slices, toasted

2 medium-ripe peaches, pitted and sliced

1 cup halved fresh blackberries

⅓ cup toasted pepitas

1. In a small bowl, whisk together the cheese, honey, cinnamon, and salt.

2. Spread 2 tablespoons of the cheese mixture on each toasted bread slice.

3. Top evenly with the peach slices, blackberries, and pepitas. Serve immediately.

Per Serving: Calories: 620; Total fat: 16g; Carbohydrates: 99g; Fiber: 8g; Protein: 24g; Sodium: 876mg

Carrot Cake Breakfast Cookies

● **DAIRY-FREE** ● **GLUTEN-FREE**

Serves 4 / **Prep time:** 5 minutes / **Cook time:** 20 minutes

Dessert that masquerades as breakfast should be a weekday requirement. These breakfast cookies are always a hit in my house, and I'm constantly changing up the add-ins. One of my favorite swaps is replacing the shredded carrots with shredded zucchini and the raisins with dark chocolate chunks. These cookies are very hearty and will keep you full all morning long with plenty of protein, carbs, and healthy fats.

¾ **cup mashed ripe banana**

1½ **cups certified gluten-free rolled oats**

1 **cup almond butter, stirred well if the oil has separated**

½ **cup chopped walnuts**

⅓ **cup honey**

1 **teaspoon pure vanilla extract**

½ **teaspoon ground cinnamon**

¼ **teaspoon sea salt**

1 **cup shredded carrots**

1 **cup raisins**

1. Preheat the oven to 325°F. Line 2 large sheet pans with parchment paper.

2. In a large bowl, combine the banana, oats, almond butter, walnuts, honey, vanilla, cinnamon, salt, carrots, and raisins. Using a rubber spatula, mix until well combined.

3. Using a ¼-cup measuring cup, scoop 6 cookies per sheet pan onto the parchment paper.

4. Using a spatula or the bottom of a glass, gently flatten the cookies.

5. Transfer the sheet pans to the oven and bake for 19 to 21 minutes, or until the cookies have lightly browned. Remove from the oven. Let cool for 5 minutes, then transfer to a wire rack to cool completely.

Tip: Cookies will stay fresh in an airtight container at room temperature for up to 1 week.

Per Serving: Calories: 877; Total fat: 47g; Carbohydrates: 105g; Fiber: 15g; Protein: 23g; Sodium: 176mg

PB&J Granola Bowls

● **SUPERFAST**

Serves 2 / **Prep time:** 5 minutes / **Cook time:** 5 minutes

If you're vegan or dairy-free, these bowls are so simple to adapt according to your dietary preferences. Simply swap out the Greek yogurt for your favorite nondairy yogurt and you're good to go. I also love using Purely Elizabeth grain-free granola instead of traditional oat granola as well. Top with fresh berries, extra peanut butter, and even a sprig of mint to make this bowl Insta-worthy.

2 cups plain Greek yogurt

¼ cup peanut butter

2 tablespoons maple syrup

1 teaspoon pure vanilla extract

½ teaspoon ground cinnamon

¼ cup strawberry jam

⅔ cup gluten-free granola

1 banana, peeled and sliced

2 tablespoons hemp hearts

1. In a bowl, stir together the yogurt, peanut butter, maple syrup, vanilla, and cinnamon until combined.

2. In a small saucepan, heat the jam over low heat for about 3 minutes, or until pourable. Remove from the heat.

3. Divide the yogurt mixture evenly between 2 bowls and top each with half of the granola, banana, and hemp hearts.

4. Top each bowl with a drizzle of jam and serve immediately.

● **Make It Faster:** I like the contrast of the warm jam and the cold yogurt, but if you're in a hurry and don't want to break out the saucepan, feel free to add a dollop of cold jam on top of the bowl.

Per Serving: Calories: 765; Total fat: 35g; Carbohydrates: 95g; Fiber: 8g; Protein: 22g; Sodium: 276mg

Cheesy Grits and Greens

● **GLUTEN-FREE**

Serves 6 / **Prep time:** 5 minutes / **Cook time:** 25 minutes

Since I'm from Kentucky, grits are a part of my DNA. On the weekends, I like to treat myself to a comforting bowl of these creamy spinach grits with a fried egg on top. If you want to make a true Southern meal, make sure there's sliced tomato on the side. Corn grits are naturally gluten-free and most brands avoid cross-contamination, but be sure to check your labels.

2 cups whole milk

3 cups water

2 teaspoons sea salt

1 teaspoon garlic powder

¼ teaspoon cayenne pepper

¼ teaspoon smoked paprika

1¼ cups old-fashioned grits

6 tablespoons unsalted butter

2 cups baby spinach

1½ cups shredded white Cheddar cheese

1. In a 6-quart pot, mix together the milk, water, salt, garlic powder, cayenne, and paprika. Bring to a boil over medium-high heat.

2. Once the mixture is boiling, whisk in the grits until smooth.

3. Reduce the heat to medium-low. Cover the pot and simmer, stirring occasionally, for 12 to 20 minutes, or until the grits have thickened.

4. Stir in the butter, spinach, and cheese until the spinach has wilted and the cheese has melted. Remove from the heat. As the grits cool, you may need to add a splash of water to thin them out. Serve hot.

● **Smart Shopping:** I prefer to shred my cheese myself since it melts better than preshredded cheese. Brands typically coat shredded cheese in an anti-clumping agent, which means the cheese doesn't melt as nicely.

Per Serving: Calories: 354; Total fat: 27g; Carbohydrates: 16g; Fiber: 1g; Protein: 11g; Sodium: 1,131mg

Garlicky Kale
and White Beans,
page 48

CHAPTER 3

Salads and Bowls

Falafel and Hummus Bowls

●**GLUTEN-FREE** ●**VEGAN**

Serves 4 to 6 / **Prep time:** 10 minutes / **Cook time:** 20 minutes

Chickpeas are a treasured legume, and even those who claim they don't like beans enjoy them. (Who doesn't love hummus?) You get a double dose of protein-rich chickpea goodness here, because in addition to the crispy baked falafel, these bowls are adorned with a healthy dose of creamy hummus. For additional nutrients and balanced protein, these bowls are lined with leafy greens and nutty quinoa.

FOR THE FALAFEL

2 (14-ounce) cans chickpeas, drained and rinsed

1 small onion, chopped

1 tablespoon minced garlic

1 teaspoon ground cumin

1½ teaspoons ground coriander

1 teaspoon baking powder

½ cup coarsely chopped fresh parsley

2 teaspoons sesame oil

1 teaspoon sea salt

FOR THE BOWLS

⅔ cup quinoa, well rinsed

1⅓ cups water

1 (5-ounce) bag mixed greens

1½ cups Green Goddess Hummus (page 147)*

TO MAKE THE FALAFEL

1. Preheat the oven to 375°F. Line a sheet pan with parchment paper.

2. Put the chickpeas, onion, garlic, cumin, coriander, baking powder, parsley, oil, and salt in a food processor. Process until well combined. The mixture will be fairly dry, but it should hold together enough to shape into small patties. Add more oil or a bit of flour if necessary.

3. Shape the mixture into 12 (2-inch) round patties.

4. Arrange the patties in a single layer on the prepared sheet pan.

5. Transfer the sheet pan to the oven and bake, turning the patties halfway through, for 20 minutes, or until golden brown. Remove from the oven.

TO MAKE THE BOWLS

6. While the patties are baking, in a medium saucepan, combine the quinoa and water. Bring to a boil over high heat.

7. Reduce the heat to medium-low. Cover the saucepan and simmer for about 15 minutes, or until the liquid has been absorbed. Remove from the heat. Let sit for a few minutes, then uncover and fluff using a fork.

8. To serve, divide the mixed greens among 4 to 6 bowls. Spoon the quinoa into one side of each bowl, top with 2 or 3 falafel, and scoop the hummus on top.

*Shortcut: If desired, you can purchase a prepared hummus in any flavor you like. Keep an eye on the ingredient list to spot any unnecessary additives.

Serving tip: Cut 2 pita breads into triangles and place them on a parchment paper-lined sheet pan. Brush them with olive oil and toast in a preheated 350°F oven for 3 to 5 minutes, or until golden brown. Arrange the pitas along the sides of the bowls.

Per Serving: Calories: 450; Total fat: 13g; Carbohydrates: 65g; Fiber: 16g; Protein: 21g; Sodium: 852mg

Buddha Bowls

● VEGAN

Serves 4 / **Prep time:** 15 minutes / **Cook time:** 10 minutes

If you've been searching for something that makes meal prep really easy at the start of the week, look no further. These pasta bowls are ideal for packing into individual containers for grab-and-go lunches. Add some crispy tofu to up the protein ante if you want to stay satiated for even longer. If you need a gluten-free soy sauce alternative, try tamari or coconut aminos, both found in the international section of the grocery store.

Sea salt

8 ounces soba or black rice noodles

⅓ cup peanut butter

1 tablespoon soy sauce

1 tablespoon freshly squeezed lime juice

2 teaspoons maple syrup

1 cup cooked shelled edamame

1 cup bean sprouts

1 cup shredded purple cabbage

3 carrots, cut into matchsticks

1 red bell pepper, chopped

¼ cup thinly sliced scallions, both white and green parts

¼ cup chopped roasted peanuts

1. Bring a large pot of salted water to a boil over high heat.

2. Cook the noodles according to the package directions. Remove from the heat. Reserving ⅓ cup of the cooking water, drain. Rinse under cold running water, then drain again.

3. To make the peanut sauce, in a small bowl, whisk together the reserved cooking water and peanut butter.

4. Add the soy sauce, lime juice, and maple syrup. Stir to combine.

5. Divide the noodles among 4 serving bowls and top each bowl with one-quarter of the edamame, bean sprouts, cabbage, carrots, and bell pepper.

6. Drizzle the bowls with the peanut sauce, then sprinkle with the scallions and peanuts.

Tip: Store this dish in an airtight container in the refrigerator for up to 4 days. If you will not be serving this dish right away, I recommend tossing the noodles with a bit of olive oil to keep them from sticking together.

Per Serving: Calories: 420; Total fat: 13g; Carbohydrates: 63g; Fiber: 5g; Protein: 20g; Sodium: 722mg

Fried Goat Cheese Salad

● **GLUTEN-FREE**
Serves 6 / **Prep time:** 15 minutes / **Cook time:** 5 minutes

When you want to wow your friends and family for brunch, this salad is the perfect solution. The warm, creamy goat cheese balances perfectly with peppery arugula and sweet grapes. Not to mention it appears way more labor intensive than it really is. Serve this masterpiece with a Jalapeño Frittata (page 18) and grapefruit mimosas for an elegant and drool-worthy Saturday spread.

1 cup gluten-free bread crumbs	1 tablespoon Dijon mustard
Sea salt	1 teaspoon minced garlic
Freshly ground black pepper	½ cup extra-virgin olive oil
1 large egg	5 ounces baby arugula
1 (10-ounce) log goat cheese, cut into 6 rounds	1 cup halved seedless red grapes
2 tablespoons avocado oil	½ red onion, thinly sliced
½ cup balsamic vinegar	¼ cup chopped toasted walnuts
2 tablespoons maple syrup	

1. Line a plate with parchment paper. Put the bread crumbs in a shallow bowl. Season with salt and pepper.

2. In another shallow bowl, beat the egg.

3. Dip each goat cheese round in the egg, then dredge in the bread crumbs to coat both sides. Put on the prepared plate.

4. In a large skillet, heat the avocado oil over medium-high heat.

5. Once the oil is hot, add the goat cheese rounds and cook for 1 to 2 minutes per side, or until browned. Remove from the heat. Transfer to the same plate.

6. To make the dressing, put the vinegar, maple syrup, mustard, and garlic in a blender. Blend until smooth.

7. With the motor running, add the olive oil in a steady stream. Season with a pinch each of salt and pepper.

8. In a large bowl, toss together the arugula, grapes, onion, walnuts, and dressing. Transfer to serving plates.

9. Top with the goat cheese rounds.

Tip: Store the dressing in an airtight container in the refrigerator for up to 5 days.

Per Serving: Calories: 499; Total fat: 37g; Carbohydrates: 28g; Fiber: 2g; Protein: 14g; Sodium: 429mg

Roasted Vegetable and Quinoa Salad

● **GLUTEN-FREE** ● **VEGAN**

Serves 4 / **Prep time:** 10 minutes / **Cook time:** 20 minutes

Roasted root vegetables combined with the warm spices of cumin, cinnamon, and cardamom are perfect for crisp fall nights—and ideal for enhancing the nutty quinoa. Feel free to add any other root vegetables you have on hand or a boost of plant-based protein such as beans, legumes, or tofu. You can also pair this salad with my Lemon-Tahini Sauce (page 149) or Crispy Garlic Chickpeas (page 148) for a complete meal.

**2 sweet potatoes, cut into
½-inch dice**

2 carrots, cut into ½-inch dice

1 tablespoon avocado oil

1 teaspoon garlic powder

1 tablespoon ground cumin

1 teaspoon ground cinnamon

¼ teaspoon sea salt

¼ teaspoon ground cardamom

2 cups water

1 cup quinoa

¼ cup golden raisins

¼ cup slivered almonds

Grated zest and juice of 1 lemon

1. Preheat the oven to 425°F. Line a sheet pan with parchment paper.

2. In a large bowl, combine the sweet potatoes, carrots, oil, garlic powder, cumin, cinnamon, salt, and cardamom. Toss well to evenly coat the vegetables with the seasoning.

3. Spread the vegetables out into an even layer on the prepared sheet pan.

4. Transfer the sheet pan to the oven and roast for about 20 minutes, or until the vegetables are soft. Remove from the oven.

5. While the vegetables are cooking, in a saucepan, combine the water and quinoa. Bring to a boil.

6. Reduce the heat to a simmer. Cook for about 15 minutes, or until the water has been absorbed. Remove from the heat.

7. In a large bowl, combine the cooked quinoa, raisins, almonds, lemon zest, and lemon juice. Toss.

8. Add the roasted vegetables and toss to combine.

9. Divide the salad among 4 bowls and serve.

Smart Shopping: Purchasing precut vegetables will save time with meal prep; however, the vegetables may still have to be cut into smaller pieces to cook within 15 minutes.

Per Serving: Calories: 334; Total fat: 10g; Carbohydrates: 55g; Fiber: 8g; Protein: 9g; Sodium: 209mg

Garlicky Kale and White Beans

● GLUTEN-FREE ● VEGAN
Serves 4 / **Prep time:** 10 minutes / **Cook time:** 10 minutes

Since kale is such a nutritional superstar, I try to work it into my diet as much as I can. Here, I've paired it with wholesome white beans and a squeeze of fresh lemon juice.

2 tablespoons extra-virgin olive oil

2 teaspoons minced garlic

¼ teaspoon red pepper flakes

1 large bunch kale, stemmed and torn

Pinch salt

Pinch freshly ground black pepper

1 (15-ounce) can white beans, drained and rinsed

Grated zest and juice of 1 lemon

3 tablespoons toasted pine nuts

1. In a large skillet, warm the oil over medium heat.

2. Add the garlic and red pepper flakes. Sauté for 1 minute, or until fragrant.

3. Add the kale. Season with the salt and black pepper. Sauté for about 4 minutes, or until wilted.

4. Add the beans and cook for 2 minutes, or until heated through.

5. Add the lemon zest and juice. Stir to combine. Remove from the heat.

6. Divide the kale and beans among 4 bowls and top each with the pine nuts before serving.

Per Serving: Calories: 223; Total fat: 12g; Carbohydrates: 24g; Fiber: 10g; Protein: 8g; Sodium: 16mg

Apple, Walnut, and Brussels Sprout Salad

● **GLUTEN-FREE** ● **SUPERFAST** ● **VEGAN**

Serves 6 / Prep time: 15 minutes

When it comes to salads, I'm truly obsessed. My number-one rule when prepping a salad is chopping up everything as small as possible. I believe that the reason some people say they don't like salad is because all they've had are large, flavorless chunks of iceberg lettuce with French dressing. Trust me when I say these ingredients chopped into small bites equal the most delicious, flavorful mouthfuls.

¼ cup white wine vinegar

1 tablespoon Dijon mustard

1 tablespoon maple syrup

½ teaspoon sea salt

1 garlic clove, finely chopped

½ cup extra-virgin olive oil

2 cups shaved Brussels sprouts

2 cups chopped lacinato kale

½ cup thinly sliced red onion

1 Honeycrisp apple, diced

⅓ cup pomegranate seeds

¼ cup walnuts

1. To make the vinaigrette, in a medium bowl, whisk together the vinegar, mustard, maple syrup, salt, and garlic.

2. Slowly stream in the oil while whisking until the mixture is smooth.

3. In a large bowl, combine the Brussels sprouts, kale, onion, apple, pomegranate seeds, and walnuts.

4. Drizzle in the desired amount of vinaigrette, toss, and serve.

Per Serving: Calories: 247; Total fat: 21g; Carbohydrates: 13g; Fiber: 3g; Protein: 2g; Sodium: 235mg

Pineapple and Coconut Tofu Bowls

● **VEGAN**

Serves 4 / **Prep time:** 15 minutes / **Cook time:** 15 minutes

Takeout is one of the hardest things to order and be confident that what you're getting is vegetarian. Instead of risking it, make these easy tofu bowls that have a delicious sweet and sour element. I like to serve them with plain white rice to make them a super easy and quick weeknight option (steam bags for the win), but you could also make creamy coconut rice to go with them.

½ cup unsweetened
   coconut flakes

½ teaspoon grated lime zest

¼ cup freshly squeezed
   lime juice

¼ cup maple syrup

½ tablespoon soy sauce

1 teaspoon cornstarch, plus
   2 tablespoons

1 (14-ounce) package
   extra-firm tofu

¼ teaspoon sea salt

2 tablespoons avocado oil

2 cups diced fresh pineapple

2 cups instant or frozen white
   rice, prepared according to the
   package directions

3 scallions, both white and
   green parts, sliced

1 ripe avocado, pitted, peeled,
   and sliced

½ cup chopped fresh cilantro

1. In a small sauté pan, toast the coconut flakes over low heat for 5 to 7 minutes, or until golden brown; keep an eye on them and stir frequently to avoid burning. Remove from the heat.

2. In a large bowl, combine the lime zest, lime juice, maple syrup, soy sauce, and 1 teaspoon of cornstarch. Whisk until the cornstarch and maple syrup are fully incorporated.

3. Drain the tofu and cut into ½-inch-wide planks. Using a paper towel, blot each plank thoroughly to dry completely. Then slice each plank into ½-inch cubes, and using a paper towel, dry again. Season with the salt.

4. In a bowl, combine the tofu and remaining 2 tablespoons of cornstarch. Toss until all the pieces are fully coated.

5. In a large skillet, heat the oil over medium heat.

6. When the oil is hot, add the tofu and panfry for 5 to 6 minutes, or until golden brown. Remove the tofu from the skillet. Set aside.

7. Reduce the heat to low. Add the maple-lime mixture to the skillet. Cook for about 3 minutes, keeping an eye on it to make sure it doesn't reduce too much.

8. Add the fried tofu and pineapple and toss to coat. Remove from the heat.

9. To serve, put ½ cup of rice in each bowl, then top with a scoop of the pineapple and tofu.

10. Top each bowl with the scallions, avocado, a sprinkle of cilantro, and toasted coconut. Serve warm.

Tip: If you have extra time, try pressing your tofu to release even more moisture. I like to place the whole block of tofu between two thick layers of clean kitchen towels with a sheet pan on top. Then use cans or other heavy objects to weigh down the sheet pan and press the tofu for 30 minutes to 1 hour before dicing. Removing as much moisture from the tofu as you can allows it to absorb the flavors of the other ingredients you're cooking with.

Per Serving: Calories: 568; Total fat: 24g; Carbohydrates: 77g; Fiber: 7g; Protein: 16g; Sodium: 280mg

Sweet and Salty Chopped Broccoli Salad

● SUPERFAST

Serves 6 / Prep time: 15 minutes

If you've ever been to a summer cookout, you've likely had a version of this salad. It's been my mom's go-to potluck contribution for years, and we always loved eating it the day after the party—we may or may not have reserved half of the salad for ourselves before even serving it to guests. The fact that it's better on day two means that you can meal prep this and have a delicious lunch all week long.

¾ **cup Greek yogurt**

½ **cup mayonnaise**

Grated zest and juice of 1 lemon

2 tablespoons white wine vinegar

¼ **cup raw cane sugar**

1¼ **teaspoons sea salt**

½ **teaspoon freshly ground black pepper**

¼ **teaspoon dry mustard**

5 cups broccoli florets, chopped into bite-size pieces

1 batch Vegetarian Bacon (page 142)*

1 cup dried cranberries

⅓ **cup sunflower seeds**

1 cup cubed Cheddar cheese

⅓ **cup chopped red onion**

1. In a large bowl, combine the yogurt, mayonnaise, lemon zest, lemon juice, vinegar, sugar, salt, pepper, and mustard. Whisk together until smooth.

2. Add the broccoli, vegetarian bacon, cranberries, sunflower seeds, cheese, and onion. Toss to combine. Serve at room temperature or chilled.

Per Serving: Calories: 537; Total fat: 40g; Carbohydrates: 38g; Fiber: 7g; Protein: 11g; Sodium: 804mg

Mushroom Fajita Bowls

● **VEGAN**

Serves 4 / **Prep time:** 10 minutes / **Cook time:** 15 minutes

Your fajitas don't have to come out on a sizzling skillet to be delicious. This homemade version uses meaty portobello mushrooms in place of chicken or steak, and let me tell you, you won't know the difference. When you're feeling tired of your typical preparation of vegetables, this is a good recipe to get you out of your rut and show you that veggies can take on so many different forms.

2 portobello mushrooms, thinly sliced

1 red bell pepper, sliced

1 yellow bell pepper, sliced

1 green bell pepper, sliced

1 red onion, sliced

2½ teaspoons fajita seasoning

3 tablespoons extra-virgin olive oil

1 cup canned black beans, drained and rinsed

2 cups instant or frozen brown rice, prepared according to the package directions

1 ripe avocado, pitted, peeled, and diced

¼ cup chopped fresh cilantro

1 lime, cut into 4 wedges

1. In a large bowl, combine the mushrooms, red bell pepper, yellow bell pepper, green bell pepper, onion, and fajita seasoning. Toss until everything is evenly coated with the seasoning mix.

2. In a large skillet, heat the oil over medium-high heat.

3. Add the seasoned vegetables and sauté for 12 to 15 minutes, or until the mushrooms are golden brown with crisp edges. Remove from the heat.

4. Meanwhile, put the beans in a microwave-safe container and microwave in 30-second intervals until just warmed through.

5. Divide the rice among 4 bowls and top with equal portions of the vegetables, beans, and avocado.

6. Top each bowl with a sprinkle of cilantro and serve with a lime wedge.

Tip: If you can't find fajita seasoning, you can make your own by combining 1 teaspoon of ground cumin, 1 teaspoon of paprika, 1 teaspoon of sea salt, 1 teaspoon of black pepper, ½ teaspoon of chili powder, ¼ teaspoon of onion powder, ¼ teaspoon of garlic powder, and ⅛ teaspoon of dried oregano. You could also use a premixed taco seasoning and add ⅛ teaspoon of dried oregano.

Per Serving: Calories: 622; Total fat: 21g; Carbohydrates: 97g; Fiber: 13g; Protein: 14g; Sodium: 147mg

Beet and Arugula Salad with Maple-Dijon Vinaigrette

● **GLUTEN-FREE** ● **SUPERFAST**

Serves 6 / Prep time: 15 minutes

Beets get a bad rap, if you ask me. Yes, the crimson-colored root vegetables have an earthy quality about them, but that's what makes them unique and delicious. My favorite way to eat them is in this very simple salad with a maple-Dijon vinaigrette, tart apple, and tangy goat cheese. Seriously, goat cheese and beets are a match made in heaven.

3 tablespoons maple syrup

2 tablespoons Dijon mustard

¼ cup balsamic vinegar

¼ teaspoon sea salt

¼ teaspoon freshly ground black pepper

¼ cup extra-virgin olive oil

10 ounces arugula

¼ cup chopped walnuts

8 ounces cooked beets, diced

1 large Granny Smith apple, sliced

2 ounces crumbled goat cheese

1. To make the vinaigrette, in a medium bowl, whisk together the maple syrup, mustard, vinegar, salt, and pepper.

2. Slowly stream in the oil while whisking until the mixture is smooth.

3. Put the arugula in a large bowl and top with the walnuts, beets, apple, and goat cheese.

4. Drizzle with the vinaigrette, then toss to combine before serving.

● **Smart Shopping:** You can roast your beets for this salad if you like, but I always have precooked beets on hand to avoid that dreaded red mess.

Per Serving: Calories: 223; Total fat: 15g; Carbohydrates: 20g; Fiber: 3g; Protein: 5g; Sodium: 244mg

Chickpea Caesar Salad

● **GLUTEN-FREE** ● **SUPERFAST** ● **VEGAN**

Serves 2 / Prep time: 15 minutes

Once upon a time, my husband and I used to go to this little café when we first moved in together. Our favorite thing on the menu was their Caesar salad, which had a unique addition of red bell pepper and peanuts. Their version used classic romaine and wasn't vegetarian friendly, but this recipe is a nod to that wonderful salad. Instead, vitamin-packed kale stands in for romaine, and the dressing is my tangy Lemon-Tahini Sauce that tastes eerily similar to Caesar but without the anchovies.

1 large bunch lacinato kale, stemmed and finely chopped

½ cup Lemon-Tahini Sauce (page 149)*

1½ cups Crispy Garlic Chickpeas (page 148)*

1 red bell pepper, thinly sliced

¼ cup chopped dry-roasted peanuts

1. Put the kale and lemon-tahini sauce in a large bowl and massage the leaves with the sauce. Let sit for 10 minutes.

2. Add the crispy chickpeas, bell pepper, and peanuts. Toss. Serve immediately.

● **Tip:** Since kale is a tougher green, it can stand up to being dressed for a while. You can store this salad in an airtight container in the refrigerator for up to 4 days, but I recommend storing the chickpeas separately to keep them crispy.

Per Serving: Calories: 349; Total fat: 21g; Carbohydrates: 31g; Fiber: 12g; Protein: 17g; Sodium: 248mg

Crispy Cabbage Bowls with Lemon-Tahini Sauce

● **GLUTEN-FREE** ● **VEGAN**

Serves 4 / **Prep time:** 10 minutes / **Cook time:** 20 minutes

One of my favorite food memories as a kid was stealing raw cabbage that my mother was prepping off the counter and snacking on it. I love cabbage and Brussels sprouts so much, and thankfully they're nutritional powerhouses with tons of fiber, antioxidants, and vitamins. This dish is so comforting and yet refreshing at the same time, which makes it perfect for a special lunch.

4 cups thinly sliced green cabbage

2 teaspoons extra-virgin olive oil

1½ teaspoons sea salt

¼ teaspoon freshly ground black pepper

½ cup Lemon-Tahini Sauce (page 149)*

2 tablespoons hemp seeds

½ cup pomegranate seeds

¼ cup chopped pistachios

1. Preheat the oven to 450°F. Line a large sheet pan with parchment paper.

2. Put the cabbage on the prepared sheet pan and drizzle with the oil. Toss to coat evenly.

3. Arrange the cabbage in an even layer. Season with the salt and pepper.

4. Transfer the sheet pan to the oven and roast, tossing halfway through, for 16 to 20 minutes, or until the cabbage is golden brown. Remove from the oven. Transfer to a large bowl.

5. Top with the lemon-tahini sauce, hemp seeds, pomegranate seeds, and pistachios. Toss to combine and serve warm.

● **Tip:** If you have a mandoline, this is the perfect recipe to break it out. Just be sure to wear a handguard to protect your fingers while shredding the cabbage.

● ***Shortcut:** You can find tahini-based dressings in most grocery stores to use in place of the Lemon-Tahini Sauce. If not, you can use a peanut sauce or a lemon vinaigrette and top with sesame seeds.

Per Serving: Calories: 254; Total fat: 18g; Carbohydrates: 18g; Fiber: 6g; Protein: 7g; Sodium: 568mg

Thai-Inspired
Sweet Potato and
Kidney Bean Soup,
page 62

CHAPTER 4

Soups, Stews, and Chilis

Thai-Inspired Sweet Potato and Kidney Bean Soup

● **GLUTEN-FREE** ● **VEGAN**

Serves 6 / **Prep time:** 5 minutes / **Cook time:** 25 minutes

Sweet potatoes not only add a delightful creaminess to this hearty soup, but also they're an especially good source of beta-carotene and vitamin C. They combine here with robust, earthy, and protein-rich kidney beans for a soup that is especially comforting and filling for cold days. If you want your soup a bit creamier, feel free to spoon half of it into a high-powered blender and blend until smooth. Combine it with the rest of the soup back in the pot, and get ready for a luscious meal.

1 (13½-ounce) can coconut milk

2 cups water, plus
   more as needed

2 shallots or 1 medium onion,
   finely chopped

2 teaspoons minced garlic

1 tablespoon minced
   fresh ginger

2 tablespoons Thai vegan red
   curry paste

1 large sweet potato, peeled
   and cut into 1-inch dice

½ teaspoon paprika

2 (14-ounce) cans kidney beans,
   drained and rinsed

2 tablespoons freshly squeezed
   lime juice

1 to 1½ teaspoons sea salt

¼ cup chopped fresh cilantro
   (optional)

1. In a large saucepan, combine the coconut milk, water, shallots, garlic, ginger, and curry paste. Bring to a boil over medium-high heat.

2. Reduce the heat to a simmer. Cook for 5 minutes to blend the flavors.

3. Add the sweet potato and simmer for 10 minutes, or until beginning to soften.

4. Stir in the paprika and beans. Simmer for 10 minutes, or until the sweet potato is fork-tender. Add more water as needed. Using the back of a spoon, mash a few of the sweet potato pieces to thicken the broth. Remove from the heat.

5. Stir in the lime juice. Season the soup with the salt, adjusting the amount to taste.

6. Serve the soup hot, garnished with the cilantro (if using).

Per Serving: Calories: 311; Total fat: 17g; Carbohydrates: 33g; Fiber: 10g; Protein: 9g; Sodium: 678mg

Mushroom-Barley Soup

Serves 6 / **Prep time:** 5 minutes / **Cook time:** 25 minutes

Yes, you can whip up a hearty, meat-free, stick-to-your-ribs soup in 30 minutes. The cooked barley helps fill you up while delivering a healthy serving of grains. Don't forget the Parmesan on top—it gives the soup a hit of salty, tangy goodness. If you're vegan, I love Follow Your Heart vegan Parmesan. And just like almost all homemade soups, this one tastes even better the next day.

2 tablespoons
  extra-virgin olive oil
1 cup chopped onion
1 cup chopped carrots
5½ cups chopped mushrooms
6 cups low-sodium
  vegetable broth
1 cup pearled barley

¼ cup red wine
2 tablespoons tomato paste
4 thyme sprigs or
  ½ teaspoon dried thyme
1 dried bay leaf
6 tablespoons grated
  Parmesan cheese

1. In a large stockpot, heat the oil over medium heat.

2. Add the onion and carrots. Cook, stirring frequently, for 5 minutes, or until the onion is translucent.

3. Increase the heat to medium-high. Add the mushrooms and cook, stirring frequently, for 3 minutes, or until softened.

4. Add the broth, barley, wine, tomato paste, thyme, and bay leaf. Stir, cover the pot, and bring to a boil.

5. Once the soup is boiling, uncover the pot to stir a few times, then reduce the heat to medium-low. Cover and cook for 12 to 15 minutes, or until the barley has cooked through. Remove from the heat.

6. Discard the bay leaf. Divide the soup among 6 soup bowls and sprinkle with the cheese.

Tip: Tomato paste is a concentrated flavor bomb that instantly makes any dish more robust. The problem is that you typically only need a few tablespoons per recipe, leaving a lot left over in the can. Spoon the remaining paste in 1-tablespoon amounts into an ice cube tray and freeze them. Once frozen, pop the cubes into a freezer bag and store them in the freezer until the next time you need tomato paste for a recipe.

Per Serving: Calories: 236; Total Fat: 7g; Carbohydrates: 35g; Fiber: 7g; Protein: 8g; Sodium: 231mg

Butternut Squash and Apple Cider Soup

● GLUTEN-FREE   ● VEGAN

Serves 6 / **Prep time:** 10 minutes / **Cook time:** 20 minutes

I've never met a butternut squash soup I didn't love, but I begin every autumn with this version. I return to it time after time because it comes together so quickly. The finishing touch of a dollop of crème fraîche is optional, but I find that it balances out the sweetness of the squash and apple cider. It can be found in the dairy case near sour cream or mascarpone in most markets.

2 tablespoons extra-virgin olive oil

2 cups diced yellow onion

10 cups diced (1-inch) butternut squash

4 cups vegetable broth

1 cup apple cider

1 teaspoon kosher salt

¼ cup crème fraîche (optional)

1 tablespoon salted sunflower seeds (optional)

1 tablespoon chopped fresh parsley (optional)

1. In a large, heavy-bottomed pot, heat the oil over medium-high heat.

2. Add the onion and sauté for about 5 minutes, or until beginning to soften.

3. Add the squash, broth, cider, and salt. Bring to a simmer. Cook for about 15 minutes, or until the squash becomes tender. Remove from the heat.

4. Using an immersion blender, puree the soup until smooth and silky. Alternatively, pour the soup into a blender (in batches if necessary) and puree.

5. Divide the soup among 6 bowls and top each with a dollop of crème fraîche (if using).

6. Garnish each with a sprinkling of sunflower seeds (if using) and parsley (if using).

Per Serving: Calories: 151; Total fat: 5g; Carbohydrates: 27g; Fiber: 5g; Protein: 2g; Sodium: 744mg

Tomato-Basil Soup with Gnocchi

● **SUPERFAST** ● **VEGAN**
Serves 4 / **Prep time:** 5 minutes / **Cook time:** 10 minutes

If you've found yourself not liking the texture of gnocchi in the past, try it in this soup. I ate this dish in a restaurant years ago and knew I had to find a way to make it at home. Jarred tomato sauce and fresh gnocchi make this the perfect quick lunch or dinner. And it's a definite step up from regular tomato soup. A grilled cheese sandwich on the side is optional but preferred.

1 tablespoon
  extra-virgin olive oil

4 cups fresh baby spinach

1 medium onion, diced

1½ teaspoons minced garlic

1 teaspoon freshly squeezed
  lemon juice

3 cups tomato-basil pasta sauce

3 cups low-sodium
  vegetable broth

1 (24-ounce) package fresh
  vegan gnocchi

2 tablespoons nutritional yeast

½ teaspoon sea salt

½ teaspoon freshly ground
  black pepper

2 tablespoons chopped fresh
  basil leaves

1. In a large pot, heat the oil over medium-high heat.

2. Add the spinach, onion, garlic, and lemon juice. Cook for 5 minutes, or until the onion is translucent and the spinach is soft.

3. Add the pasta sauce and broth. Bring to a simmer.

4. Add the gnocchi and cook for 3 minutes, or until tender. Remove from the heat.

5. Stir in the nutritional yeast. Season with the salt and pepper.

6. Divide the soup among 4 bowls, garnish with the basil, and serve.

Tip: For some extra richness, stir in 2 to 3 tablespoons of coconut cream or soy cream into each bowl before serving.

Per Serving: Calories: 375; Total fat: 16g; Carbohydrates: 48g; Fiber: 7g; Protein: 11g; Sodium: 744mg

Pumpkin and White Bean Chili

● **GLUTEN-FREE** ● **VEGAN**

Serves 6 / **Prep time:** 5 minutes / **Cook time:** 25 minutes

As soon as you feel that first crisp chill in the air, it's time to break out this chili. Whether you're potlucking for a tailgate or hosting everyone for the big game, this dish will please meat eaters and vegans alike. I love creamy white beans in this soup, but you can substitute kidney, pinto, or black beans for them as well. My perfect secret side dish? A classic peanut butter sandwich.

3 tablespoons
extra-virgin olive oil

1 onion, diced

2 carrots, diced

2 celery stalks, diced

2 garlic cloves, minced

1 tablespoon ground coriander

1 tablespoon smoked paprika

1 teaspoon ground cumin

2 teaspoons sea salt

½ teaspoon freshly ground
black pepper

1 (7-ounce) can diced
green chiles

1 (15-ounce) can unsweetened
pumpkin puree

1 (15-ounce) can fire-roasted
diced tomatoes

2 (15-ounce) cans cannellini
beans, drained and rinsed

2 cups low-sodium
vegetable broth

1. In a large pot, heat the oil over medium heat.

2. Add the onion, carrots, and celery. Cook, stirring occasionally, for 5 minutes, or until the vegetables have softened.

3. Add the garlic, coriander, paprika, cumin, salt, and pepper. Cook for 1 minute.

4. Add the green chiles, pumpkin puree, tomatoes with their juices, beans, and broth. Stir to combine. Bring to a simmer. Cook for 15 to 19 minutes, or until slightly thickened. Remove from the heat. Adjust the seasonings as needed. Serve warm.

Tip: This chili makes for the perfect freezer meal for a rainy day! Once the chili has cooled, pour into freezer bags and lay flat in the freezer to freeze, making them easier to store. Freeze for up to 3 months.

Per Serving: Calories: 228; Total fat: 8g; Carbohydrates: 33g; Fiber: 5g; Protein: 9g; Sodium: 862mg

Tortilla Soup with Quinoa

● **VEGAN**

Serves 6 / **Prep time:** 5 minutes / **Cook time:** 25 minutes

Tortilla soup is one of those comforting dishes that warms you from the inside out. I added quinoa to bump up the nutrition and make this soup more filling for long-lasting fuel. In addition to the tortilla strips, you can top with sliced radish, pickled jalapeños, and diced avocado to serve. This one is so fun to set up as a bar with all the toppings so everyone can choose their own!

1 tablespoon
  extra-virgin olive oil

3 garlic cloves, minced

1 onion, diced

1 green bell pepper, diced

½ teaspoon sea salt

½ teaspoon freshly ground
  black pepper

2 tablespoons tomato paste

1 tablespoon chili powder

1½ teaspoons ground cumin

1 teaspoon dried oregano

6 cups vegetable broth

1 (28-ounce) can diced
  tomatoes

1 (15-ounce) can black beans,
  drained and rinsed

1½ cups frozen corn

½ cup quinoa

Juice of 1 lime

½ cup chopped fresh cilantro

1 cup tortilla strips

1. In a large pot, heat the oil over medium heat.

2. Add the garlic, onion, bell pepper, salt, and black pepper. Cook, stirring occasionally, for 3 to 4 minutes, or until tender.

3. Stir in the tomato paste, chili powder, cumin, and oregano. Cook for about 1 minute, or until fragrant.

4. Stir in the broth, diced tomatoes with their juices, beans, corn, and quinoa. Bring to a boil.

5. Reduce the heat to a simmer. Cook for 15 to 20 minutes, or until the quinoa is tender. Remove from the heat.

6. Stir in the lime juice and cilantro.

7. Divide the soup among 6 bowls and top with the tortilla strips and any additional desired toppings. Serve immediately.

Smart Shopping: You can find tortilla strips in the section with the salad toppings in the grocery store. If you can't find them, you can crush up tortilla chips or make your own! Simply cut corn tortillas into strips; drizzle with a tiny bit of olive oil, chili powder, salt, and pepper; and bake at 375°F for 10 to 12 minutes.

Per Serving: Calories: 245; Total fat: 5g; Carbohydrates: 43g; Fiber: 10g; Protein: 10g; Sodium: 449mg

Curried Carrot and Ginger Soup

● **GLUTEN-FREE** ● **VEGAN**

Serves 4 / **Prep time:** 10 minutes / **Cook time:** 20 minutes

This luscious, velvety soup is so full of flavor, you won't believe there's a quarter pound of carrots per serving. Between the carrots and sweet potatoes, your eyes are screaming for joy from the beta-carotene. Toppings are essential for soups, in my opinion, and for this one, I love to swirl in coconut cream, sprinkle on toasted pepitas, and add a dash of paprika to finish for color.

1 tablespoon coconut oil

1 white onion, diced

3 garlic cloves, minced

2 tablespoons minced fresh ginger

2 teaspoons yellow curry powder

1 teaspoon paprika

1 teaspoon sea salt

½ teaspoon freshly ground black pepper

1 pound carrots, diced

2 small sweet potatoes, peeled and diced

2½ cups vegetable broth

½ cup full-fat coconut milk

Juice of 1 lime

1. In a large pot, heat the oil over medium-high heat.

2. Add the onion and sauté for 2 to 3 minutes, or until translucent.

3. Add the garlic and ginger. Sauté for 1 minute, or until soft.

4. Add the curry powder, paprika, salt, and pepper. Sauté for 1 minute, or until fragrant.

5. Add the carrots and sweet potatoes, then pour in the broth. Bring to a boil.

6. Reduce the heat to low. Cover the pot and simmer for about 15 minutes, or until the carrots and sweet potatoes are fork-tender.

7. Add the coconut milk and lime juice. Remove from the heat. Working in batches, carefully transfer the soup to a high-powered blender and puree until smooth. Taste and adjust the seasonings as needed before serving.

Tip: If you have an immersion blender, this is the perfect opportunity to get some use out of it. Simply puree the soup directly in the pot in step 7 before serving.

Per Serving: Calories: 212; Total fat: 10g; Carbohydrates: 30g; Fiber: 7g; Protein: 3g; Sodium: 702mg

Lentil and Root Vegetable Stew

● **VEGAN**

Serves 6 / **Prep time:** 10 minutes / **Cook time:** 20 minutes

If a soup could be a warm blanket, it would be this one. It has slow-cooked flavor from the concentrated tomato paste, herbs, and aromatics but comes together in no time. Just imagine bringing this to work for lunch and dreaming about it all morning. You have to serve it with a hunk of crusty bread for dipping, or better yet, serve in a bread bowl so you can devour the whole thing.

2 tablespoons extra-virgin olive oil

1 yellow onion, diced

2 carrots, diced

1 parsnip, diced

2 garlic cloves, minced

2 tablespoons tomato paste

1 russet potato, peeled and diced

2 (15-ounce) cans stewed tomatoes

1 (15-ounce) can lentils, drained and rinsed

½ teaspoon paprika

½ teaspoon dried thyme

½ teaspoon dried oregano

½ teaspoon freshly ground black pepper

4 cups vegetable broth

2 tablespoons soy sauce

1. In a large pot, heat the oil over medium heat.

2. Add the onion, carrots, parsnip, and garlic. Sauté for about 4 minutes, or until the onion is translucent.

3. Add the tomato paste. Cook for 2 to 3 minutes, or until fragrant.

4. Add the potato, stewed tomatoes with their juices, lentils, paprika, thyme, oregano, pepper, and broth. Stir to combine. Cover the pot and bring to a boil.

5. Reduce the heat to low. Simmer for about 15 minutes, or until the potato is fork-tender. Remove from the heat.

6. Stir in the soy sauce, then taste and adjust the seasonings as needed.

Smart Shopping: Precooked lentils are available in the canned foods section with the rest of the legumes. They come canned, in microwaveable pouches, and even vacuum sealed in the produce section.

Per Serving: Calories: 214; Total fat: 5g; Carbohydrates: 36g; Fiber: 10g; Protein: 8g; Sodium: 490mg

Creamy Vegetable and Rice Soup

Serves 6 / **Prep time:** 10 minutes / **Cook time:** 20 minutes

What's more comforting than a big bowl of creamy rice soup, just like Mom used to make? Although this soup is amazing when you have the sniffles, don't let its magic be reserved for when you're not feeling great. I love adding chopped mushrooms to this dish when I have them around and serving this with old-school saltine crackers. Now you just need a fuzzy robe and slippers, and you're good to go.

¼ cup extra-virgin olive oil

1 cup diced yellow onion

1¼ cups diced celery

1¼ cups diced carrot

1 tablespoon chopped fresh thyme leaves

1½ teaspoons sea salt

1½ teaspoons freshly ground black pepper

3 garlic cloves, minced

¼ cup all-purpose flour

4 cups instant or frozen white rice, prepared according to the package directions

8 cups vegetable broth

2 cups water

1 cup heavy (whipping) cream

1. In a large pot, heat the oil over medium-high heat.

2. Add the onion, celery, carrot, thyme, salt, and pepper. Stir to combine. Cook, stirring occasionally, for 6 minutes, or until the onion is translucent.

3. Add the garlic and cook for about 1 minute, or until fragrant.

4. Reduce the heat to medium. Sprinkle the flour over the vegetables and stir to coat. Cook for 3 minutes, or until the flour turns light brown.

5. Add the rice, broth, and water, stirring quickly to prevent lumps. Cover the pot and bring to a simmer. Cook for 10 minutes, or until slightly thickened. Remove from the heat.

6. Stir in the cream. Divide the soup among 6 bowls and serve immediately.

Tip: My favorite vegan alternative to heavy cream for this soup is cashew cream. To make it, soak ¾ cup of raw cashews overnight, drain, then blend in a high-powered blender with ¼ cup of water until smooth. Stir into the soup in step 6 before serving.

Per Serving: Calories: 739; Total fat: 25g; Carbohydrates: 116g; Fiber: 5g; Protein: 11g; Sodium: 632mg

Miso Mushroom Ramen

● **DAIRY-FREE**

Serves 4 / **Prep time:** 5 minutes / **Cook time:** 25 minutes

Going out for ramen is one of my favorite treats. So much flavor can be packed into one bowl of brothy, fragrant goodness. The main flavor component of this dish is white miso, which is found in the refrigerated section of the health food aisle or the international aisle in most grocery stores. I highly recommend picking up a container since it's great to use in everything, from chocolate chip cookies to this ramen, for a burst of flavor.

¼ cup extra-virgin olive oil

2 pounds shiitake mushrooms, coarsely chopped

2 garlic cloves, minced

1½ teaspoons red pepper flakes (use less for less heat)

6 cups vegetable broth

2 cups water

¼ cup low-sodium soy sauce

2 tablespoons rice vinegar

3 tablespoons white miso

2 tablespoons minced fresh ginger

2 heads baby bok choy, halved

3 (3-ounce) packages ramen noodles (discard any seasoning packets, or save for use in another recipe)

¼ cup chopped fresh cilantro

4 soft-boiled eggs (optional)

½ cup shredded carrots (optional)

4 scallions, both white and green parts, chopped (optional)

1. In a large pot, heat the oil over medium heat.

2. Add the mushrooms, garlic, and red pepper flakes. Sauté for about 5 minutes, or until the mushrooms begin to brown.

3. Add the broth, water, soy sauce, vinegar, miso, ginger, and bok choy. Bring to a low boil.

4. Reduce the heat to medium-low. Simmer for 15 minutes, or until the bok choy is tender.

5. Stir in the noodles and cilantro. Cook for 5 minutes, or until the noodles are soft. Remove from the heat.

6. Divide the noodles and soup among 4 bowls. Top each with half the bok choy, a soft-boiled egg (if using), carrots (if using), and scallions (if using).

Per Serving: Calories: 512; Total fat: 26g; Carbohydrates: 59g; Fiber: 9g; Protein: 15g; Sodium: 1,832mg

Cucumber-Herb Gazpacho

● **GLUTEN-FREE** ● **SUPERFAST** ● **VEGAN**

Serves 4 / Prep time: 10 minutes

Everyone always talks about how great soup is for cold weather. Although I agree, there's nothing like a well-chilled summer gazpacho. This bright green version is full of antioxidants, vitamins, and minerals to leave you feeling bright and energized. This soup is perfect to make ahead and keep chilled in the refrigerator for a few days. I like to reblend and add more salt if needed before serving.

1 large cucumber, peeled, seeded, and coarsely chopped

1 cup baby spinach

3 celery stalks, coarsely chopped

¼ cup torn fresh basil leaves

2 tablespoons chopped fresh mint

2 tablespoons chopped fresh parsley

1 garlic clove, chopped

2 tablespoons freshly squeezed lemon juice

⅓ cup extra-virgin olive oil

½ cup coconut yogurt

1½ cups cold water

1 teaspoon sea salt

⅛ teaspoon freshly ground black pepper

Put the cucumber, spinach, celery, basil, mint, parsley, garlic, lemon juice, oil, yogurt, water, salt, and pepper in a high-powered blender. Puree until smooth. Taste and adjust the seasonings as needed. Chill until ready to serve, or add ice cubes to chill the soup quickly to your desired temperature.

Per Serving: Calories: 210; Total fat: 18g; Carbohydrates: 10g; Fiber: 1g; Protein: 2g; Sodium: 626mg

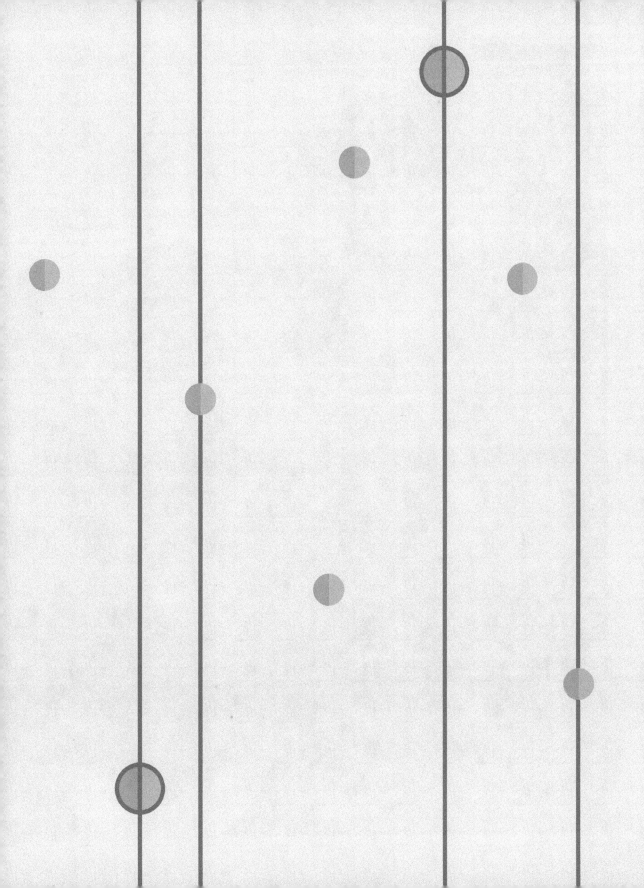

**VLT Sandwiches,
page 88**

CHAPTER 5

Handhelds

Open-Faced Pesto and Provolone Melts

● SUPERFAST
Serves 4 / **Prep time:** 5 minutes / **Cook time:** 10 minutes

Your grilled cheese game just got taken up a notch with these fancy knife-and-fork sandwiches. The pesto-mayo combo accentuates the toppings and tends to be a winner with family members of any age, meat eaters or not. For a cozy night in, serve with Tomato-Basil Soup with Gnocchi (page 68).

8 bread slices (ciabatta, baguette, or focaccia are great choices)

8 tablespoons mayonnaise

8 tablespoons Cashew-Basil Pesto (page 143)*

4 jarred roasted red peppers, halved lengthwise

8 tomato slices, halved

1 cup fresh spinach

8 tablespoons diced red onion

8 provolone cheese slices

1. Preheat the oven to 400°F.

2. Put the bread slices on a sheet pan.

3. Slather each bread slice with 1 tablespoon of mayonnaise and 1 tablespoon of pesto.

4. Top with a roasted red pepper half, 2 tomato halves, and a few spinach leaves.

5. Sprinkle each slice with 1 tablespoon of diced red onion, then top each with 1 cheese slice.

6. Transfer the sheet pan to the oven and bake for 5 minutes, or until the cheese begins to melt.

7. Set the oven to broil. Broil for about 2 minutes, or until the cheese is bubbling. Remove from the oven. Serve the sandwiches open faced.

● *Shortcut: Any store-bought pesto you like is just fine! My absolute favorite is the Vegan Kale, Cashew, and Basil Pesto from Trader Joe's, even for nonvegans. I buy a couple of containers at a time and freeze portions in ice trays for later use.

Per Serving: Calories: 925; Total fat: 61g; Carbohydrates: 62g; Fiber: 4g; Protein: 33g; Sodium: 1,789mg

VLT Sandwiches

● **DAIRY-FREE**   ● **SUPERFAST**
Serves 4 / **Prep time:** 15 minutes

VLTs are what I turn to when I need a quick meal that doesn't require a lot of effort. If you grew up eating traditional BLTs, then this recipe will trigger all the nostalgia. You won't believe how fabulous the smoky homemade "bacon" is—you won't be able to have a salad or veggie burger without it from now on!

¼ **cup mayonnaise**
8 bread slices, toasted
1 large tomato, sliced

8 romaine lettuce leaves
½ **batch Vegetarian Bacon (page 142)***

1. Spread the mayonnaise on each of the toasted bread slices.

2. Top 4 bread slices with equal amounts of the tomato, lettuce, and bacon.

3. Cover each with the remaining bread slices, mayonnaise-side down, and serve.

● ***Shortcut:** To save time, purchase vegetarian bacon from the store. You can find it in the refrigerated section of most grocery stores, often near the produce with vegan cheese and other meat substitutes.*

Per Serving: Calories: 436; Total fat: 23g; Carbohydrates: 49g; Fiber: 6g; Protein: 10g; Sodium: 592mg

Garden Vegetable Wraps

● **SUPERFAST** ● **VEGAN**

Serves 4 / **Prep time:** 10 minutes

These healthy wraps come together in a flash and are packed with delicious ingredients that will leave you feeling great. For a little extra protein, add cooked or canned beans, crumbled steamed tempeh, or your favorite chopped nuts. Leftover roasted veggies are also so delicious paired with the hummus. I like to serve these with blue corn tortilla chips and some fresh Pico de Gallo (page 151) for dipping.

½ cup Green Goddess Hummus (page 147)*

4 large whole-wheat wraps

2 cups chopped romaine lettuce

1½ cups shredded purple cabbage

1 red bell pepper, diced

¼ cup chopped cherry tomatoes

¼ cup alfalfa sprouts

2 ripe avocados, pitted, peeled, and sliced

1. Spread one-quarter of the hummus onto each wrap.

2. Evenly divide the lettuce, cabbage, bell pepper, tomatoes, alfalfa sprouts, and avocados among the wraps.

3. Tuck the sides of each wrap in, then roll tightly into a burrito. Secure using toothpicks to keep the wraps closed if not serving right away, but be sure to remove the toothpicks before consuming.

● **Make It Faster:** This is a perfect recipe to use meal-prepped veggies. Cut the vegetables and store them in an airtight container in the refrigerator for up to 4 days. Wait to cut the avocados until just before preparing the wraps.

Per Serving: Calories: 416; Total fat: 20g; Carbohydrates: 51g; Fiber: 12g; Protein: 11g; Sodium: 706mg

Southwestern Egg Rolls

Serves 6 / **Prep time:** 10 minutes / **Cook time:** 20 minutes

Here's a surprisingly easy vegetarian version of a take-out favorite with a unique Southwestern twist. I bake these egg rolls, but you can also fry them until golden brown. Serve them alone or with a tangy dipping sauce like Cilantro-Lime Crema (page 150) or a spicy salsa verde.

Nonstick cooking spray

1 (15-ounce) can black beans, drained and rinsed

1 jalapeño, seeded and diced

1 red bell pepper, diced

1 cup frozen corn, thawed

1 cup shredded Cheddar cheese

1 tablespoon chili powder

1 teaspoon ground cumin

Pinch salt

Pinch freshly ground black pepper

12 egg roll wrappers

1. Preheat the oven to 400°F. Line a rimmed sheet pan with parchment paper. Coat well with cooking spray.

2. To make the filling, in a large bowl, toss together the beans, jalapeño, bell pepper, corn, cheese, chili powder, and cumin. Season with salt and black pepper.

3. Coat the egg roll wrappers with cooking spray.

4. Divide the filling equally among the wrappers and roll them according to the package directions.

5. Place the egg rolls, seam-side down, on the prepared sheet pan and coat the tops with cooking spray.

6. Transfer the sheet pan to the oven and bake for 15 to 20 minutes, or until the egg rolls are golden brown. Remove from the oven.

Per Serving: Calories: 288; Total fat: 7g; Carbohydrates: 45g; Fiber: 6g; Protein: 13g; Sodium: 432mg

Mediterranean Pita Pizzas with Olives and Goat Cheese

Serves 2 / **Prep time:** 5 minutes / **Cook time:** 10 minutes

Pita bread makes up the crust for these quick and easy mini pizzas that can be served as a dinner alongside a green salad or as a colorful lunch or snack.

2 (7-inch) pita bread rounds

¾ cup prepared tomato sauce

½ red onion, thinly sliced

½ cup sliced pitted black or Kalamata olives

4 ounces goat cheese, cut into discs

2 tablespoons extra-virgin olive oil

½ teaspoon dried oregano

½ teaspoon red pepper flakes

1. Preheat the oven to 400°F.

2. Put the pita bread in the oven and warm for 1 minute. Remove them from the oven, leaving the oven on. Put on a sheet pan.

3. Spread half of the tomato sauce onto each pita.

4. Divide the onion, olives, and goat cheese between the pitas.

5. Drizzle 1 tablespoon of oil over each pita, then sprinkle with the oregano and red pepper flakes.

6. Transfer the sheet pan to the oven and bake for 6 to 8 minutes, or until the edges have just started to brown and crisp. Remove from the oven. Transfer the pitas to a cutting board.

7. Cut the pitas into wedges and serve.

Per Serving: Calories: 419; Total fat: 24g; Carbohydrates: 40g; Fiber: 4g; Protein: 11g; Sodium: 674mg

Spicy Black Bean and Sweet Potato Sliders

● **VEGAN**

Serves 6 / **Prep time:** 5 minutes / **Cook time:** 25 minutes

Black bean burgers are my favorite way to change up my bean game. The sweet potatoes give the burgers a slightly sweet flavor that's offset with a Southwestern kick of spices. Get creative and add any leftover veggies you have on hand to your patties. I like to top the finished sliders with a little avocado and lots of hot sauce. Feel free to double the recipe and freeze the extras—they're perfect for a quick meal any time of day!

2 medium sweet potatoes

1 (15-ounce) can black beans, drained and rinsed

1 cup instant or frozen brown rice, prepared according to the package directions

½ small red onion, finely diced

2 teaspoons ground cumin

1 teaspoon smoked paprika

¼ teaspoon sea salt

¼ teaspoon chili powder

12 whole-wheat slider buns

2 ripe avocados, pitted, peeled, and cut into ¼-inch dice

2 tablespoons hemp seeds

2 tablespoons chipotle hot sauce

1. Preheat the oven to 400°F. Line a sheet pan with parchment paper.

2. Using a fork, pierce the sweet potatoes 3 or 4 times. Microwave, turning halfway through, for 5 minutes. Let cool slightly.

3. Meanwhile, put the beans in a medium bowl. Using a potato masher or fork, mash to a slightly chunky consistency.

4. Add the rice, onion, cumin, paprika, salt, and chili powder. Stir well.

5. Carefully spoon the flesh out of the cooled sweet potatoes and add it to the bean mixture. Stir well.

6. Roll the sweet potato–bean mixture into 12 (1½-inch) balls.

7. Arrange the balls on the prepared sheet pan and flatten them to about ½-inch thickness.

8. Transfer the sheet pan to the oven and bake for 10 minutes. Flip the patties and bake for 10 more minutes, or until golden brown. Remove from the oven.

9. Serve the patties on the buns. Top with the avocados, hemp seeds, and hot sauce.

Per Serving: Calories: 458; Total fat: 12g; Carbohydrates: 71g; Fiber: 16g; Protein: 19g; Sodium: 563mg

Cannellini Bean Lettuce Wraps with Green Goddess Hummus

● **GLUTEN-FREE** ● **SUPERFAST** ● **VEGAN**

Serves 6 / **Prep time:** 5 minutes / **Cook time:** 10 minutes

Lettuce wraps are easy to make and extremely versatile as an appetizer or lunch—you can stuff them with anything from nutritious grains to egg salad. Plus, they're a terrific option for those who follow a gluten-free lifestyle. For this Mediterranean spin, I slather on Green Goddess Hummus and then spoon a warm, buttery bean filling onto crisp leaves of romaine lettuce.

1 tablespoon
    extra-virgin olive oil

½ cup diced red onion

¾ cup chopped fresh tomatoes

¼ teaspoon freshly ground
    black pepper

1 (15-ounce) can cannellini or
    Great Northern beans, drained
    and rinsed

¼ cup finely chopped fresh
    curly parsley

½ cup Green Goddess Hummus
    (page 147)*, divided

8 romaine lettuce leaves

1. In a large skillet, heat the oil over medium heat.

2. Add the onion and cook, stirring occasionally, for 3 minutes, or until translucent.

3. Add the tomatoes and pepper. Cook, stirring occasionally, for 3 minutes, or until the tomatoes release their juices.

4. Add the beans and cook, stirring occasionally, for 3 minutes, or until warmed through. Remove from the heat.

5. Mix in the parsley.

6. Spread 1 tablespoon of hummus over each lettuce leaf.

7. Evenly spread the warm bean mixture down the center of each leaf.

8. Fold one side of each lettuce leaf lengthwise over the filling, then fold over the other side to make a wrap and serve.

*Shortcut: Use your favorite store-bought hummus if you're short on time.

Smart Shopping: Leafy romaine is my go-to choice for lettuce wraps because of its long leaves and sturdy yet pleasantly crisp, edible stems. Other options are green leaf, red leaf, Boston, or Bibb lettuces. You can also use heartier greens like kale, cabbage, Swiss chard, and collards; they just need to be parboiled or steamed before wrapping.

Per Serving: Calories: 211; Total fat: 8g; Carbohydrates: 28g; Fiber: 8g; Protein: 10g; Sodium: 368mg

Cauliflower Banh Mi

Serves 2 / **Prep time:** 10 minutes / **Cook time:** 20 minutes

Banh mi are one of my favorite handheld eats because of their mix of fresh, cooked, and pickled flavors. Cauliflower is my go-to choice for making them vegetarian, but you could also use the same marinade for tofu or tempeh and it would be amazing. Traditionally, Vietnamese baguettes are used to make a banh mi, but if you can't find them, any small baguette, hoagie, or sandwich-size roll will work.

2 tablespoons chili-garlic sauce

3 tablespoons low-sodium soy sauce

1 tablespoon maple syrup

1 tablespoon freshly squeezed lime juice

1 tablespoon avocado oil

4 cups fresh cauliflower florets, cut into bite-size pieces if large

¼ cup Cilantro-Lime Crema (page 150)*

2 small baguettes, toasted and split

¼ cup Pickled Red Onions (page 144)**

⅓ cup shredded carrots

½ small English cucumber, thinly sliced

2 tablespoons chopped fresh cilantro

1. In a medium mixing bowl, whisk together the chili-garlic sauce, soy sauce, maple syrup, lime juice, and oil.

2. Add the cauliflower and toss until coated evenly.

3. Heat a large skillet with a lid over medium-high heat.

4. Using a slotted spoon, scoop the cauliflower into the skillet, reserving the leftover liquid. Sauté, stirring occasionally, for about 5 minutes, or until slightly browned.

5. Reduce the heat to medium. Add the reserved marinade and toss to coat. Cook for about 15 minutes, or until the cauliflower is tender. Remove from the heat.

6. To assemble the sandwiches, spread the crema on the cut sides of the baguettes.

7. Divide the cauliflower between the bottoms of the baguettes, then top with the pickled red onions, carrots, cucumber, and cilantro.

8. Cover with the tops of the baguettes and serve.

*Shortcut: Any good-quality mayonnaise or vegan mayonnaise would work here in place of the Cilantro-Lime Crema.

**Shortcut: Substitute fresh thinly sliced red onion, or use a jarred pickled vegetable mix for that pickled flavor.

Per Serving: Calories: 591; Total fat: 21g; Carbohydrates: 83g; Fiber: 10g; Protein: 19g; Sodium: 1,987mg

Margherita Pizza Rolls

Serves 6 / **Prep time:** 15 minutes / **Cook time:** 15 minutes

This is a fun Friday dinner that the whole family can get involved in. Everyone likes getting their hands in dough from time to time! If you have both meat eaters and vegetarians in the family, you can make a few different fillings based on everyone's preferences. Another favorite veggie filling is smearing on Cashew-Basil Pesto (page 143) as a base and filling with leftover roasted veggies and shredded provolone cheese.

1 tablespoon all-purpose flour

1 (1-pound) package premade pizza dough, at room temperature

1 tablespoon extra-virgin olive oil

½ teaspoon sea salt

¼ teaspoon freshly ground black pepper

½ teaspoon garlic powder

¼ teaspoon dried oregano

½ cup shredded mozzarella cheese

12 to 15 fresh basil leaves

8 to 10 cherry tomatoes, halved

1 large egg, whisked

1. Dust your work surface with the flour.

2. Divide the dough into 2 portions. Roll out each portion into a rectangle of about 9 by 11 inches.

3. Brush the surface of the dough with the oil. Season with the salt, pepper, garlic powder, and oregano.

4. Evenly sprinkle the cheese over each pizza, and arrange the basil and tomatoes in an even layer over the cheese.

5. With the longest side toward you, roll the dough tightly like a log, pressing as you go to secure. When you get to the end, pinch the seam to seal. Repeat with the other pizza dough, then transfer the logs to a plate and freeze for 10 minutes.

6. While the dough chills, preheat the oven to 400°F. Line a sheet pan with parchment paper.

7. Using a sharp knife, cut each log into 1-inch-thick pinwheels.

8. Place the pinwheels 2 inches apart on the prepared sheet pan.

9. Brush the top of each pinwheel with the egg.

10. Transfer the sheet pan to the oven and bake for 15 minutes, or until the pinwheels are golden brown and the cheese has melted. Remove from the oven.

Smart Shopping: Premade pizza dough comes in a few different forms and sizes. You can usually buy a 1-pound bag of dough or a roll that comes in a can in the refrigerated section, similar to biscuits or crescent rolls. If you buy the kind that's prerolled, you won't split the dough in half, you'll just unroll it, add the filling, and roll it back up before freezing and slicing.

Per Serving: Calories: 253; Total fat: 7g; Carbohydrates: 37g; Fiber: 2g; Protein: 10g; Sodium: 699mg

Roasted Eggplant Panini with Romesco Sauce

Serves 4 / **Prep time:** 10 minutes / **Cook time:** 20 minutes

Sometimes you want a sandwich for lunch that's more elevated than the simple grilled cheese that's usually available to vegetarians. This roasted eggplant sandwich feels like an upscale delicatessen treat but is easy to prepare at home with a few simple ingredients. If you don't love eggplant, roasted portobello mushrooms or zucchini would be delicious in its place.

2 small eggplants, cut into ¼-inch-thick slices

2 tablespoons extra-virgin olive oil

1 tablespoon sea salt

2 tablespoons chopped fresh rosemary leaves

8 focaccia bread slices

4 tablespoons Romesco Sauce (page 146)*

8 provolone cheese slices

1. Preheat the oven to 450°F.

2. Coat both sides of the eggplant slices with the oil, salt, and rosemary.

3. Arrange the eggplant in a single layer on a sheet pan.

4. Transfer the sheet pan to the oven and roast, turning halfway through, for 15 minutes, or until the eggplant is tender. Remove from the oven, leaving the oven on.

5. Reduce the oven temperature to 400°F.

6. Lay out 4 bread slices and top each slice with 1 tablespoon of romesco sauce, 1 cheese slice, 3 or 4 roasted eggplant slices, another cheese slice, and the remaining bread slices.

7. Put the sandwiches on the sheet pan.

8. Return the sheet pan to the oven and toast for about 5 minutes, or until the bread has lightly browned and the cheese has melted. Remove from the oven and serve.

*Shortcut: Several brands sell romesco sauce at major grocery stores, but you could also use your favorite jarred marinara sauce in a pinch.

Per Serving: Calories: 464; Total fat: 24g; Carbohydrates: 43g; Fiber: 10g; Protein: 22g; Sodium: 2,612mg

Chickpea Pita with Lemon-Tahini Sauce

● **SUPERFAST** ● **VEGAN**
Serves 4 / Prep time: 10 minutes

The simple Lemon-Tahini Sauce in this recipe is so creamy, tangy, and heavenly, you'll find all kinds of uses for it. Juicy chopped tomatoes and crunchy, tart pickles add texture and flavor to these wraps. To switch up the recipe, you can buy frozen falafels or make them from my Falafel and Hummus Bowls recipe (page 40) and use them on the pitas in place of the chickpeas for a truly delicious meal.

1 (14-ounce) can chickpeas, drained and rinsed

1½ cups Lemon-Tahini Sauce (page 149)*

1 teaspoon ground cumin

8 (7-inch) pita bread rounds

2 medium-firm tomatoes, chopped

½ cup chopped dill pickles

¼ cup chopped fresh parsley leaves

1. Put the chickpeas in a mixing bowl and mash using a fork or potato masher.

2. Stir in the lemon-tahini sauce and cumin.

3. Divide the chickpea mixture between the pitas. Top with the tomatoes, pickles, and parsley.

● ***Shortcut:** You can also use a store-bought tahini-based sauce instead of the Lemon-Tahini Sauce, or switch it up by mixing plain Greek yogurt with some lemon juice and garlic to top these wraps.

Per Serving: Calories: 583; Total fat: 14g; Carbohydrates: 94g; Fiber: 10g; Protein: 22g; Sodium: 932mg

Bean and Cheese Flautas

Serves 2 / **Prep time:** 10 minutes / **Cook time:** 10 minutes

When Taco Tuesday just isn't doing it for you anymore, these warm and gooey flautas are the perfect way to shake up your dinner routine. If you're gluten-free, a corn tortilla would be the perfect substitute for flour tortillas. Just be sure you're picking up refried beans that are specifically vegetarian.

1 (16-ounce) can vegetarian refried beans

2 tablespoons Pico de Gallo (page 151)*, plus more for serving

½ teaspoon chili powder

½ teaspoon garlic powder

½ teaspoon ground cumin

½ cup shredded pepper Jack cheese

6 medium flour tortillas

2 tablespoons avocado oil

Guacamole, for serving

1. In a large bowl, combine the beans, pico de gallo, chili powder, garlic powder, cumin, and cheese.

2. Spread about 3 tablespoons of the bean mixture on the bottom half of each tortilla.

3. Roll each tortilla away from you tightly, leaving the sides open.

4. In a large skillet, heat the oil over medium-high heat. Line a plate with paper towels.

5. Place half of the flautas, seam-side down, in the skillet. Cook, turning every 30 seconds or so, for about 2 minutes, or until golden and crispy on all sides. Transfer to the prepared plate to drain. Repeat with the remaining flautas. Remove from the heat.

6. Serve the flautas warm with guacamole and additional pico de gallo.

Per Serving: Calories: 759; Total fat: 29g; Carbohydrates: 94g; Fiber: 14g; Protein: 31g; Sodium: 1,846mg

**Walnut Pesto
Zoodles, page 120**

CHAPTER 6

Mains

Easy Pad Thai

● **DAIRY-FREE**

Serves 4 / **Prep time:** 15 minutes / **Cook time:** 15 minutes

If you love pad Thai as much as I do, you'll want to try this easy variation on the traditional dish. With crunchy vegetables in a creamy peanut sauce, it's both sweet and savory, and you'll find yourself making it all the time without even thinking about it. This recipe is easily enhanced with frozen edamame or crispy tofu for added protein or any leftover veggies you have in the refrigerator.

Sea salt

8 ounces pad Thai noodles

2 large eggs

¼ teaspoon freshly ground black pepper, plus a pinch

Nonstick cooking spray, for coating the skillet

¼ cup peanut butter

1 tablespoon soy sauce

1 tablespoon freshly squeezed lime juice

1 tablespoon grated fresh ginger

2 teaspoons raw cane sugar

2 bell peppers, sliced

1 cup shredded purple cabbage

⅓ cup chopped peanuts

¼ cup chopped fresh cilantro

1. Bring a large pot of salted water to a boil over high heat.

2. Cook the noodles according to the package directions. Remove from the heat. Reserving ¼ cup of the cooking water, drain the noodles and transfer to a large bowl.

3. In a small bowl, beat the eggs. Season with ¼ teaspoon of salt and the black pepper.

4. Coat a large skillet with cooking spray and heat over medium heat.

5. Add the eggs and cook undisturbed for about 3 minutes, or until just set. Remove from the heat. Transfer to a plate and cut into large pieces.

6. To make the peanut sauce, in a medium bowl, whisk together the reserved cooking water and peanut butter.

7. Add the soy sauce, lime juice, ginger, and sugar. Season the sauce with a pinch each of salt and black pepper.

8. To the bowl with the noodles, add the egg, bell peppers, cabbage, and peanut sauce. Toss.

9. Top with the peanuts and cilantro. Serve.

Tip: Store this pad Thai in an airtight container in the refrigerator for up to 3 days.

Per Serving: Calories: 434; Total fat: 17g; Carbohydrates: 59g; Fiber: 5g; Protein: 14g; Sodium: 280mg

Avocado Pesto Pasta

● **VEGAN**

Serves 4 / **Prep time:** 5 minutes / **Cook time:** 25 minutes

Basil adds fragrant flavor to dishes, but did you know this aromatic herb is also an excellent source of vitamin K? Additionally, basil contains essential oils and phytochemicals to help fight inflammation. Speaking of vitamin K, asparagus is full of it, along with iron, zinc, riboflavin, and folate. Who knew? This fresh, nutty pasta dish is not only a summertime hit but also will help keep you feeling your best.

Sea salt

8 ounces whole-wheat penne

3 tablespoons chopped fresh parsley

3 tablespoons chopped fresh basil leaves

2 tablespoons chopped fresh chives

3 tablespoons freshly squeezed lemon juice

½ cup mashed ripe avocado

3 large garlic cloves, smashed

Pinch freshly ground black pepper

2 tablespoons extra-virgin olive oil, divided

1 bunch asparagus, trimmed and quartered

1 pint cherry tomatoes

Fresh basil leaves, for garnish

1. Bring a large pot of salted water to a boil over high heat.

2. Cook the penne according to the package directions. Remove from the heat. Reserving ½ cup of the cooking water, drain.

3. To make the pesto, put the parsley, basil, chives, lemon juice, avocado, garlic, ½ teaspoon of salt, the pepper, 1 tablespoon of oil, and ¼ cup of the reserved cooking water in a high-powered blender. Blend, scraping down the sides as needed, until smooth.

4. In a deep 12-inch skillet, heat the remaining 1 tablespoon of oil over medium heat.

5. Add the asparagus and sauté for 4 minutes.

6. Add the tomatoes and ⅛ teaspoon of salt. Sauté for 5 minutes, or until the asparagus is soft.

7. Add the cooked penne and pesto. Gradually add the remaining ¼ cup of cooking water and cook for about 4 minutes, or until well combined and the pesto adheres to the penne. Remove from the heat.

8. Divide the pasta among 4 bowls and serve topped with basil.

Tip: Whenever making pasta, save ¼ to ½ cup of the cooking water before draining. Adding the cooking water when combining the pasta and sauce will allow the sauce to better coat the pasta.

Per Serving: Calories: 399; Total fat: 18g; Carbohydrates: 53g; Fiber: 10g; Protein: 14g; Sodium: 106mg

Penne with Indian-Style Tomato Sauce and Mushrooms

● **VEGAN**

Serves 4 / **Prep time:** 5 minutes / **Cook time:** 25 minutes

Ginger and garam masala give this tomato pasta sauce a spicy and enticing Indian character. Ginger is one of nature's healthiest spices, providing many scientifically proven benefits, including aiding digestion and reducing inflammation. Garam masala is an aromatic Indian spice blend that, like many other international ingredients, has gained attention and popularity lately and can be found in most supermarkets. This unique dish is one you're going to crave time after time.

2 tablespoons extra-virgin olive oil

1 (8-ounce) package sliced white mushrooms

2 tablespoons minced fresh ginger

2 tablespoons minced garlic

½ tablespoon garam masala

¼ teaspoon red pepper flakes

1 (28-ounce) can crushed or diced tomatoes

Sea salt

3 cups penne

1. In a medium saucepan, heat the oil over medium heat.

2. When the oil is hot, add the mushrooms and sauté for 5 minutes, or until beginning to soften.

3. Add the ginger, garlic, garam masala, and red pepper flakes. Cook, stirring, for 3 minutes.

4. Stir in the tomatoes with their juices and ½ teaspoon of salt. Bring to a boil, being careful of splattering.

5. Reduce the heat to a simmer. Cook for 10 minutes, or until the sauce thickens. Remove from the heat.

6. While the sauce is simmering, bring a large pot of salted water to a boil.

7. Cook the penne according to the package directions. Remove from the heat. Drain and return to the pot.

8. Stir in the tomato sauce. Serve hot.

Tip: Two inches of fresh ginger provides an intense ginger flavor. Peel the root using a paring knife, then grate it using a fine cheese grater. Or, to save time, use jarred minced ginger.

Tip: If you don't have garam masala, combine ½ teaspoon of ground cumin, ½ teaspoon of freshly ground black pepper, and ¼ teaspoon of ground cinnamon to substitute.

Per Serving: Calories: 326; Total fat: 9g; Carbohydrates: 52g; Fiber: 9g; Protein: 11g; Sodium: 306mg

Coconut Cauliflower and Spinach over Rice Noodles

● **GLUTEN-FREE** ● **VEGAN**

Serves 4 / **Prep time:** 10 minutes / **Cook time:** 20 minutes

This is one of those dishes that tastes so divine that, when sitting down to enjoy it, you would think it was complicated. But don't be fooled. This dish of tender cauliflower, fresh spinach, and tomato simmered in a fragrant coconut milk sauce comes together in hardly any time at all, and it's a great way to get a big helping of nourishing vegetables. It smells and tastes just as wonderful as it looks.

2½ **tablespoons extra-virgin olive oil, divided**

2 **cups fresh cauliflower florets**

½ **tablespoon minced garlic**

1 **jalapeño, seeded and finely chopped**

1 **(14-ounce) can coconut milk**

1 **large tomato, diced**

½ **teaspoon ground cumin**

½ **teaspoon ground turmeric (optional)**

4 **cups water**

8 **ounces rice noodles**

1 **(5-ounce) bag fresh spinach, chopped**

1 **teaspoon sea salt**

1. In a large saucepan, heat 2 tablespoons of oil over medium-high heat.

2. Add the cauliflower, garlic, and jalapeño. Cook, stirring, for 2 minutes, or until the garlic and jalapeño are fragrant.

3. Pour in the coconut milk and bring to a simmer.

4. Add the tomato, cumin, and turmeric (if using).

5. Reduce the heat to medium. Cover the saucepan and simmer, stirring occasionally, for 5 to 10 minutes, or until the sauce begins to thicken and the cauliflower is fork-tender

6. While the cauliflower and tomato are cooking, in a medium sauce-pan, bring the water to a boil.

7. Stir in the noodles and cover the saucepan. Remove from the heat. Let sit for 5 minutes (or up to 10 minutes for wider rice noodles). Drain and transfer to a bowl.

8. Add the spinach to the saucepan with the cauliflower and tomato, a few handfuls at a time, and stir until the spinach has wilted. Simmer for 5 minutes, or until the flavors have combined.

9. Stir in the salt. Remove from the heat.

10. Stir the remaining ½ tablespoon of oil into the noodles and trans-fer to 4 serving plates.

11. Spoon the cauliflower, spinach, and tomato mixture over each por-tion and serve immediately.

Tip: Two cups of prepared riced cauliflower can be used in place of cau-liflower florets for a creamier sauce. Add the riced cauliflower in step 8 with the spinach instead of in step 2.

Per Serving: Calories: 386; Total fat: 31g; Carbohydrates: 27g; Fiber: 5g; Protein: 6g; Sodium: 675mg

Spaghetti with Mushroom Bolognese

● **VEGAN**

Serves 6 / **Prep time:** 10 minutes / **Cook time:** 20 minutes

Minced mushrooms take the place of ground beef in this flavorful vegetarian version of classic spaghetti Bolognese. The sauce is very thick and has relatively little tomato, much as you would find in Italy rather than in Italian restaurants in North America. And like in Italy, the sauce is stirred into the pasta before serving. No matter where you are, this is a favorite of vegetarians and nonvegetarians alike.

2½ tablespoons extra-virgin olive oil, divided

1½ pounds cremini mushrooms, minced

1 red onion, finely chopped

1 large carrot, finely chopped

2 garlic cloves, minced

Sea salt

1 pound spaghetti

1 large tomato, finely chopped

2 tablespoons tomato paste

1¼ cups red cooking or drinking wine

2 teaspoons balsamic or red wine vinegar

2 teaspoons dried oregano

1. In a nonstick skillet, heat 2 tablespoons of oil over medium-high heat.

2. Add the mushrooms, onion, carrot, and garlic. Cook, stirring often, for 10 minutes, or until the mushrooms have browned. Transfer to a bowl.

3. While the mushrooms are cooking, bring a large pot of salted water to a boil over high heat.

4. Add the spaghetti to the pot and cook until al dente, according to the package directions. Remove from the heat. Reserving ½ cup of the cooking water, drain. Rinse the pasta quickly with cold water and return it to the pot.

5. In the same skillet used to cook the mushrooms, heat the remaining ½ tablespoon of oil over medium heat.

6. Add the tomato, tomato paste, wine, vinegar, oregano, and 1½ teaspoons of salt. Cook, stirring occasionally, for 5 minutes.

7. Stir in the mushroom mixture and reserved cooking water. Simmer, stirring often, for 5 minutes, or until the sauce has thickened. Remove from the heat.

8. Pour the sauce into the pot with the spaghetti and stir well to coat. Serve hot.

Make It Faster: Put coarsely chopped mushrooms, onion, carrot, and garlic in a blender or food processor and pulse until the mushrooms and vegetables resemble coarse crumbs. Be careful not to overprocess.

Per Serving: Calories: 394; Total fat: 7g; Carbohydrates: 63g; Fiber: 10g; Protein: 13g; Sodium: 410mg

Cannellini Bean Ratatouille

● GLUTEN-FREE ● VEGAN
Serves 4 / **Prep time:** 10 minutes / **Cook time:** 20 minutes

Ratatouille is a French stew typically made with summer vegetables, including zucchini, eggplant, tomatoes, onion, and garlic. And, no, you don't need the help of a talented rat chef to make this dish. It can be enjoyed hot or cold and is usually served as a side dish. I like to add white beans and pine nuts along with a hearty slice of bread to make it a complete meal. Bon appétit!

2 tablespoons extra-virgin olive oil

½ yellow onion, chopped

3 garlic cloves, minced

2 tablespoons tomato paste

1 zucchini, cut into 1-inch dice

1 small yellow squash, cut into 1-inch dice

1 small eggplant, cut into 1-inch dice

¼ cup water

½ teaspoon sea salt

⅛ teaspoon freshly ground black pepper

1 (15-ounce) can fire-roasted diced tomatoes

1 (15-ounce) can cannellini beans, drained and rinsed

¼ cup chopped fresh basil leaves

¼ cup pine nuts (optional)

¼ cup chopped olives (optional)

1. In a large, deep skillet, heat the oil over medium heat.

2. Add the onion, garlic, and tomato paste. Sauté for 2 minutes, or until the onion is translucent.

3. Add the zucchini, squash, and eggplant. Sauté for 4 minutes.

4. Add the water and mix well, scraping the bottom of the skillet to loosen any browned bits. Cook for 4 minutes.

5. Add the salt, pepper, diced tomatoes with their juices, and beans. Cook for 10 minutes, or until the sauce has reduced.

6. Stir in the basil. Remove from the heat.

7. Divide the ratatouille among 4 bowls. Add the pine nuts (if using) and olives (if using). Serve.

Tip: This dish can also be baked in the oven at 425°F for 25 minutes. Simply spray a baking dish with nonstick cooking spray, then combine all the ingredients in the dish. Leftovers can be stored in an airtight container in the refrigerator for up to 5 days.

Per Serving: Calories: 302; Total fat: 15g; Carbohydrates: 35g; Fiber: 12g; Protein: 10g; Sodium: 662mg

Cauliflower Gratin

● **GLUTEN-FREE** ● **VEGAN**

Serves 4 / **Prep time:** 5 minutes / **Cook time:** 25 minutes

If you still think plant-based meals are boring, this Cauliflower Gratin is here to change your mind. This gooey, cheesy dish topped with a crispy crumb topping will become your go-to comfort food. This versatile dish works for a satisfying main course or even an appetizer or side dish for a crowd. Feel free to add some spinach or kale to get your greens in, but beware—your guests might not want to share it!

Nonstick cooking spray, for coating the baking dish

3 cups bite-size fresh cauliflower florets

1¾ cups raw cashews, divided

¼ teaspoon sea salt, divided

3 tablespoons hemp seeds

¼ teaspoon dried parsley

1 tablespoon nutritional yeast, plus ¼ cup

1½ teaspoons garlic powder, divided

1½ teaspoons onion powder, divided

¾ cup plain unsweetened almond milk

1 cup vegetable broth

3 tablespoons almond flour

1 teaspoon ground cumin

1. Preheat the oven to 400°F. Spray a 9-inch square baking dish with nonstick cooking spray.

2. Put the cauliflower in a medium saucepan and cover with water. Bring to a boil over high heat.

3. Reduce the heat to a simmer. Cook for 5 minutes, or until the cauliflower is al dente. Remove from the heat. Drain and transfer to a large bowl.

4. While the cauliflower is cooking, to make the cashew topping, put 1 cup of cashews, ⅛ teaspoon of salt, the hemp seeds, parsley, 1 tablespoon of nutritional yeast, ½ teaspoon of garlic powder, and ½ teaspoon of onion powder in a food processor or high-speed blender. Blend until finely chopped. Remove the mixture from the food processor and set aside.

5. To make the cashew cheese, put the remaining ¾ cup of cashews, ¼ cup of nutritional yeast, 1 teaspoon of garlic powder, 1 teaspoon of onion powder, the almond milk, broth, almond flour, cumin, and remaining ⅛ teaspoon of salt in the food processor. Blend until smooth.

6. Pour the cashew cheese over the cauliflower and combine well.

7. Pour the mixture into the prepared baking dish and cover with the cashew topping.

8. Transfer the baking dish to the oven and bake for 20 minutes, or until the gratin is golden brown and bubbly. Remove from the oven.

9. Divide the gratin among 4 bowls and serve hot.

● **Tip:** If you don't have a high-speed blender, cover the cashews with water in a saucepan and boil for about 15 minutes to soften. Drain and transfer to a traditional blender with the remaining ingredients in step 5 to blend the cashew cheese.

Per Serving: Calories: 429; Total fat: 32g; Carbohydrates: 26g; Fiber: 5g; Protein: 17g; Sodium: 357mg

Walnut Pesto Zoodles

● GLUTEN-FREE

Serves 4 / **Prep time:** 10 minutes / **Cook time:** 10 minutes

Even the lifelong pasta obsessed can benefit from the occasional swap of a zoodle. What else are you going to do with all of those zucchini from your garden this summer? If you don't want to invest in a spiralizer, the good news is that most grocery stores now sell spiralized veggies in the produce section or freezer department. You'll be a convert to the zoodle life in no time with this version.

4 medium zucchini or 8 cups prespiralized zoodles

4 tablespoons extra-virgin olive oil, divided

2 garlic cloves, minced, divided

½ teaspoon red pepper flakes

¼ teaspoon freshly ground black pepper, divided

¼ teaspoon sea salt, divided

2 tablespoons grated Parmesan cheese, divided

1 cup packed fresh basil leaves

¾ cup walnut pieces, divided

1. Make the zucchini noodles (zoodles) using a spiralizer or your vegetable peeler (run the peeler down the length of the zucchini to make long strips).

2. In a large bowl, gently combine the zoodles, 1 tablespoon of oil, 1 minced garlic clove, the red pepper flakes, ⅛ teaspoon of black pepper, and ⅛ teaspoon of salt.

3. In a large skillet, heat ½ tablespoon of oil over medium-high heat.

4. Add half of the zoodles and cook, stirring every minute or so, for 5 minutes. Transfer to a large serving bowl. Repeat with another ½ tablespoon of oil and the remaining zoodles. Remove from the heat. Transfer to the serving bowl.

5. If using a food processor to make the pesto, add the remaining minced garlic clove, ⅛ teaspoon of black pepper, ⅛ teaspoon of salt, 1 tablespoon of cheese, the basil, and ¼ cup of walnuts. Process, and with the machine running, slowly drizzle the remaining 2 tablespoons of oil into the opening until the pesto is completely blended.

6. If using a high-powered blender, put the 2 tablespoons of oil in the blender first and then add the rest of the pesto ingredients. Pulse until the pesto is completely blended.

7. Add the pesto, remaining 1 tablespoon of cheese, and ½ cup of walnuts to the zoodles. Mix well and serve.

⬤ **Make It Faster:** Short on time? Make a big batch of Cashew-Basil Pesto (page 143) ahead and use that in a pinch!

Per Serving: Calories: 310; Total fat: 29g; Carbohydrates: 10g; Fiber: 4g; Protein: 7g; Sodium: 207mg

Spicy Cauliflower Tacos with Blue Cheese

● **GLUTEN-FREE**

Serves 4 / **Prep time:** 10 minutes / **Cook time:** 20 minutes

I am a sucker for anything spicy. As the sole heat lover in my household, I usually have to resort to dousing my food in hot sauce and red pepper flakes or meal prepping my spicy delight to have as lunch throughout the week. These Buffalo-inspired tacos are so full of flavor, not to mention they're packed with fiber and antioxidants from nutrient-powerhouse cauliflower. If you thought cauliflower's moment in the spotlight was over, think again.

3 tablespoons unsalted butter

3 tablespoons gluten-free
  hot sauce

1 large head cauliflower,
  cut into florets

1 tablespoon
  extra-virgin olive oil

8 corn tortilla shells

1 cup shredded red cabbage

1 cup halved cherry tomatoes

1 ripe avocado, pitted, peeled,
  and sliced

½ cup crumbled blue cheese

¼ cup chopped fresh parsley

⅓ cup Avocado Ranch Dressing
  (page 145)*

1. Preheat the oven to 400°F. Line a sheet pan with parchment paper.

2. In a small saucepan, melt the butter over medium-low heat. Remove from the heat. Transfer to a medium bowl.

3. Add the hot sauce to the bowl and combine to make the Buffalo sauce.

4. In a large bowl, combine the cauliflower, oil, and half of the Buffalo sauce. Toss to coat.

5. Spread the cauliflower out on the prepared sheet pan.

6. Transfer the sheet pan to the oven and roast for 20 minutes, or until the cauliflower is fork-tender and browned. Remove from the oven. Transfer to the bowl with the remaining Buffalo sauce and toss.

7. Wrap the tortilla shells in a damp paper towel and heat in the microwave for 30 seconds. Or heat one at a time in a dry pan over low heat for 30 seconds per side.

8. Layer the cabbage, cauliflower, tomatoes, avocado, cheese, and parsley into the tortilla shells.

9. Drizzle each taco with the ranch dressing and serve.

*Shortcut: Any store-bought gluten-free ranch dressing will work. You can also buy a packet of ranch seasoning and add it to plain Greek yogurt to taste. Thin with a bit of water and serve in place of the Avocado Ranch Dressing.

Per Serving: Calories: 503; Total fat: 35g; Carbohydrates: 41g; Fiber: 12g; Protein: 13g; Sodium: 607mg

French Onion Rigatoni

Serves 6 / **Prep time:** 10 minutes / **Cook time:** 20 minutes

It can be difficult deciding on a dish to make for a date-night-in that doesn't seem like every other weeknight meal. This rich and creamy pasta is here to make your life easier and your partner very happy. The flavor that you get here tastes like it took triple the time it actually takes to make this dish. The trick is the slow addition of the vegetable broth and the honey that cooks down into the onions and caramelizes them to perfection.

4 tablespoons (½ stick) unsalted butter

2 teaspoons honey

2 or 3 medium yellow onions, thinly sliced

½ cup vegetable broth

Sea salt

1 pound rigatoni

2 garlic cloves, minced

2 tablespoons chopped fresh thyme leaves

¼ teaspoon freshly ground black pepper

1 tablespoon soy sauce

¼ teaspoon cayenne pepper

1¼ cups heavy (whipping) cream

½ cup shredded Gruyère cheese

1. In a large pot, melt the butter over medium-high heat.

2. Stir in the honey and onions. Cook, stirring occasionally, for about 5 minutes, or until the onions have softened.

3. Slowly add the broth ¼ cup at a time, until it begins to reduce. Cook for 8 to 10 minutes, or until the onions are deeply caramelized.

4. While the onions are cooking, bring a large pot of salted water to a boil.

5. Add the rigatoni to the boiling water and cook until al dente, according to the package directions. Remove from the heat. Drain.

6. To the caramelized onions, add the garlic, thyme, ½ teaspoon of salt, and the black pepper. Cook for 3 to 4 minutes.

7. Stir in the soy sauce, cayenne, cream, and cheese.

8. Fold in the cooked rigatoni until fully coated. Remove from the heat. Serve hot.

Per Serving: Calories: 582; Total fat: 30g; Carbohydrates: 64g; Fiber: 3g; Protein: 14g; Sodium: 491mg

Eggplant Parmesan Pasta Bake

Serves 6 / **Prep time:** 5 minutes / **Cook time:** 25 minutes

Who doesn't love eggplant Parm? Unfortunately, there's the issue of having to dredge each slice in egg, flour, and bread crumbs and then frying individually. Frankly, no one has time for that on a weeknight. This cheater pasta bake gives you that scratch-made Italian flavor and cheesy topping you love in a simple no-fuss package. Opt for whole-wheat pasta to make this one even more filling and nutritious.

Nonstick cooking spray, for coating the baking dish

1 tablespoon extra-virgin olive oil

4 garlic cloves, minced

¼ teaspoon dried oregano

⅛ teaspoon red pepper flakes

1 large eggplant, peeled and diced

1 (24-ounce) jar marinara sauce

½ cup vegetable broth

Sea salt

½ teaspoon freshly ground black pepper

1 pound rotini

1 cup grated Parmesan cheese, divided

1 cup shredded mozzarella cheese

¼ cup chopped fresh basil leaves

1. Preheat the oven to 475°F. Spray a 9-by-12-inch baking dish with cooking spray.

2. In a large skillet, combine the oil, garlic, oregano, and red pepper flakes. Cook over medium heat for about 1 minute, or until fragrant.

3. Add the eggplant and sauté for 3 minutes, or until beginning to soften.

4. Stir in the marinara sauce, broth, 1 teaspoon of salt, and the black pepper. Bring to a simmer. Cook for 10 to 12 minutes, or until the sauce has thickened.

5. While the eggplant is cooking, bring a large pot of salted water to a boil over high heat.

6. Add the rotini to the boiling water and cook until al dente, according to the package directions. Remove from the heat. Drain.

7. Once the sauce has simmered for 10 minutes, add the cooked rotini and stir to fully coat.

8. Stir in ¾ cup of Parmesan cheese. Remove from the heat. Transfer to the prepared baking dish.

9. Sprinkle the mozzarella cheese and remaining ¼ cup of Parmesan cheese over the top.

10. Transfer the baking dish to the oven and bake for 10 minutes, or until the cheese has melted. Remove from the oven.

11. Serve the pasta bake warm, topped with the basil.

Per Serving: Calories: 480; Total fat: 13g; Carbohydrates: 71g; Fiber: 7g; Protein: 21g; Sodium: 825mg

Hot Honey Corn Ribs

● **DAIRY-FREE** ● **GLUTEN-FREE**
Serves 4 / **Prep time:** 5 minutes / **Cook time:** 25 minutes

Do not adjust your glasses: You read that right. If you've ever felt left out of a summer barbecue because you're a vegetarian, these "ribs" will change all of that. All you need to transform a humble corncob into finger-licking-good vegan ribs is a sharp knife. Could you use this same recipe on whole corncobs? Sure. But sometimes it's nice to have fun with your food to make you feel like you're on the same page as your carnivorous friends.

2 ears of corn, shucked and silk removed

1 tablespoon extra-virgin olive oil

1 teaspoon chili powder

1 teaspoon paprika

½ teaspoon garlic powder

1 teaspoon dried oregano

1 teaspoon sea salt

¼ teaspoon freshly ground black pepper

½ cup honey

1 teaspoon red pepper flakes

1½ teaspoons apple cider vinegar

½ cup Cilantro-Lime Crema (page 150) (optional)

1. Preheat the oven to 375°F. Line a sheet pan with parchment paper.

2. Using a sharp knife, cut each ear of corn into 4 ribs: Slice down the center lengthwise, then cut each of those halves in half lengthwise again.

3. Put the corn ribs on the prepared sheet pan. Drizzle the ribs with the oil and sprinkle with the chili powder, paprika, garlic powder, oregano, salt, and black pepper. Using your hands, massage the spices into the corn.

4. Transfer the sheet pan to the oven and bake for 20 to 25 minutes, or until the corn ribs have fully cooked. Remove from the oven.

5. While the corn is baking, to make the hot honey, whisk together the honey, red pepper flakes, and vinegar in a small bowl.

6. Drizzle the corn ribs with the hot honey and serve with the crema (if using).

Tip: When cooking corn ribs in the oven, they tend to stay straight. If you have an air fryer at home and want that curled look of a natural rib, the air fryer is the way to go. Simply heat your air fryer to 400°F and place the corn ribs in a single layer in the basket. Cook for 10 to 15 minutes, or until curled and golden brown.

Per Serving: Calories: 226; Total fat: 4g; Carbohydrates: 50g; Fiber: 3g; Protein: 3g; Sodium: 614mg

Burrito-Stuffed Bell Peppers

Serves 6 / **Prep time:** 5 minutes / **Cook time:** 25 minutes

I remember being so confused by stuffed peppers as a kid whenever my mom would make them. She would cut just the top stem off the bell pepper, fill it completely full, and bake them standing up. It made for a wow presentation, but it was not easy to eat. These stuffed peppers are sliced in half lengthwise, so you get two halves per person and they cook much quicker.

1 tablespoon extra-virgin olive oil

½ yellow onion, diced

1 (14-ounce) can diced tomatoes

2 tablespoons taco seasoning

1 (14-ounce) can black beans, drained and rinsed

1 cup frozen corn

3 cups instant or frozen brown rice, prepared according to the package directions

3 large bell peppers, halved lengthwise

1 cup shredded pepper Jack cheese

3 scallions, both white and green parts, chopped

½ cup chopped fresh cilantro

1. Preheat the oven to 400°F.

2. In a large skillet, heat the oil over medium heat.

3. Add the onion and sauté for about 3 minutes, or until translucent.

4. Add the tomatoes with their juices, taco seasoning, beans, corn, and rice. Stir to combine. Remove from the heat.

5. Place the bell pepper halves, cut-side up, in a 9-by-13-inch baking dish.

6. Fill the peppers with the rice mixture and top with the cheese.

7. Transfer the baking dish to the oven and bake for 20 minutes, or until the bell pepper is tender and the cheese has melted. Remove from the oven.

8. Top with the scallions and cilantro. Serve.

Tip: I love turning these stuffed peppers into stuffed pepper "nachos"! Instead of standard bell peppers, use a bag of mini bell peppers for a two-bite treat. Just fill them the same way and bake for 8 to 10 minutes.

Per Serving: Calories: 583; Total fat: 12g; Carbohydrates: 100g; Fiber: 12g; Protein: 18g; Sodium: 414mg

Cranberry-Jalapeño Swedish "Meatballs"

Serves 6 / **Prep time:** 5 minutes / **Cook time:** 25 minutes

If you were a meat eater in a previous life, you may find yourself craving those famous meatballs from IKEA. Although this vegetarian version has a sweet and spicy twist, it still hits all the same bells and whistles. These are perfect served over your favorite creamy mashed potatoes or buttered egg noodles with a dollop of homemade cranberry sauce on the side.

2 cups cooked brown rice

¾ cup finely chopped mushrooms

¼ cup finely chopped dried cranberries

1 jalapeño, seeded and minced

1 cup plain Greek yogurt, divided

2 large eggs

¾ cup plain bread crumbs

1 teaspoon smoked paprika

1 teaspoon garlic powder

1 teaspoon sea salt, divided

3 tablespoons unsalted butter

½ teaspoon onion powder

3 tablespoons all-purpose flour

1½ cups vegetable broth

¼ teaspoon freshly ground black pepper

1. Preheat the oven to 425°F. Line a sheet pan with parchment paper.

2. In a large bowl, mix together the rice, mushrooms, cranberries, jalapeño, ½ cup of yogurt, the eggs, bread crumbs, paprika, garlic powder, and ½ teaspoon of salt.

3. Roll about 2 tablespoons of the mixture into a ball, then place on the prepared sheet pan. Repeat with the remaining mixture.

4. Transfer the sheet pan to the oven and bake for 15 to 20 minutes, or until the meatballs are firm. Remove from the oven.

5. While the meatballs are baking, in a large skillet, melt the butter over medium-low heat.

6. Add the onion powder and flour. Cook, stirring constantly, for 1 minute, or until the mixture forms a paste.

7. Whisking continuously, slowly add the broth.

8. Whisk in the remaining ½ cup of yogurt. Season with the remaining ½ teaspoon of salt and the pepper.

9. Add the cooked meatballs and toss to coat. Remove from the heat. Serve warm.

Per Serving: Calories: 259; Total fat: 10g; Carbohydrates: 35g; Fiber: 3g; Protein: 8g; Sodium: 529mg

Vegetable Lo Mein with Tofu

● **VEGAN**

Serves 4 / **Prep time:** 10 minutes / **Cook time:** 20 minutes

Your typical take-out order has nothing on this simple and easy lo mein. The great thing is that you can add whatever vegetables you have in the refrigerator or freezer to make it a breeze. I love to stock up on frozen stir-fry veggies for just this occasion. Mushrooms are another go-to add-in for all the B vitamins, as are edamame for protein and snow peas for vitamin C and fiber.

1½ tablespoons sesame oil, divided

1 (14-ounce) package extra-firm tofu, dried using paper towels and cut into ½-inch cubes

1 teaspoon garlic powder

Sea salt

8 ounces lo mein or linguine

¼ cup soy sauce

1 tablespoon pure maple syrup

1 tablespoon rice vinegar

1 onion, thinly sliced

2 garlic cloves, minced

½ cup shredded carrots

1 large red bell pepper, julienned

3 scallions, both white and green parts, sliced

1. In a large skillet, heat 1 tablespoon of oil over high heat.

2. Add the tofu and cook, stirring occasionally, for 8 to 10 minutes, or until golden and lightly crispy. Season with the garlic powder and ¼ teaspoon of salt. Remove from the heat. Transfer to a plate.

3. While the tofu is cooking, bring a large pot of salted water to a boil over high heat.

4. Add the lo mein and cook until al dente, according to the package directions. Remove from the heat. Drain.

5. To make the sauce, in a small bowl, whisk together the soy sauce, maple syrup, and vinegar.

6. In the skillet used to cook the tofu, heat the remaining ½ tablespoon of oil over medium heat.

7. Add the onion and stir-fry for 3 minutes, or until browned around the edges.

8. Add the garlic, carrots, and bell pepper. Cook for 4 minutes, or until the vegetables are tender.

9. Add the noodles and sauce and toss well to combine.

10. Add the tofu and scallions and toss once more. Remove from the heat. Serve hot.

Smart Shopping: You can find lo mein in the Asian section of most grocery stores. If you can't find them, you can swap in soba noodles or even spaghetti or linguine. Just make sure you follow the directions on the package for cook times.

Per Serving: Calories: 459; Total fat: 20g; Carbohydrates: 54g; Fiber: 4g; Protein: 17g; Sodium: 1,713mg

Kale and Mushroom Strata

Serves 6 / **Prep time:** 5 minutes / **Cook time:** 20 minutes

I love a dish that can wake up and be breakfast but also moonlight as a fun dinner. Traditionally, strata and bread pudding are cooked at a lower temperature for a longer time. Here, I'm raising the temperature a touch to make it speedy, but you'll still get that pillowy texture. This strata is pure comfort food and will leave you feeling so satisfied.

Nonstick cooking spray, for coating the baking dish

5 large eggs

½ cup heavy (whipping) cream

½ cup half-and-half

½ cup diced white onion

8 ounces shredded Gruyère cheese

8 ounces shredded Monterey Jack cheese

1 teaspoon Dijon mustard

1 teaspoon sea salt

½ teaspoon freshly ground black pepper

6 cups cubed (¾-inch) crusty bread, such as a baguette

8 ounces cremini mushrooms, cut into ¼-inch-thick slices

2 cups chopped lacinato kale

1. Preheat the oven to 425°F. Spray a 9-by-9-inch baking dish with cooking spray.

2. In a large bowl, whisk together the eggs, cream, half-and-half, onion, Gruyère, Monterey Jack, mustard, salt, and pepper.

3. Gently stir in the bread, mushrooms, and kale. Transfer to the prepared baking dish.

4. Transfer the baking dish to the oven and bake for 22 minutes, or until the strata has browned and completely set.

....

Per Serving: Calories: 561; Total fat: 38g; Carbohydrates: 23g; Fiber: 2g; Protein: 31g; Sodium: 1,145mg

Homestyle Vegetable Potpie

Serves 4 / Prep time: 10 minutes / **Cook time:** 20 minutes

If Cracker Barrel had a vegetarian potpie on their menu, this would be it. It's creamy and hearty with a pillowy biscuit crust that warms you from the inside out. You might be surprised to see cream of mushroom soup in the ingredients, but as long as you're reading labels, it's a great option on busy nights. You can also sub with cream of cauliflower soup if you like.

Nonstick cooking spray, for coating the pie plate

1 (10-ounce) can organic cream of mushroom soup

1 cup milk of choice, divided

1 cup frozen mixed peas and carrots

1 cup frozen corn

1 (14-ounce) can chickpeas, drained and rinsed

½ teaspoon sea salt

½ teaspoon freshly ground black pepper

½ teaspoon garlic powder

1 large egg

1 cup biscuit mix

1. Preheat the oven to 400°F. Spray a 9-inch pie plate with cooking spray.

2. In a large bowl, combine the cream of mushroom soup, ½ cup of milk, the peas and carrots, corn, and chickpeas. Season with the salt, pepper, and garlic powder. Mix, then transfer to the prepared pie plate.

3. In a small bowl, stir together the remaining ½ cup of milk, the egg, and biscuit mix until no lumps remain. Spread evenly over the vegetable mixture.

4. Transfer the pie plate to the oven and bake for 20 minutes, or until the topping is golden brown. Remove from the oven. Let stand 10 minutes before serving.

Per Serving: Calories: 404; Total fat: 14g; Carbohydrates: 57g; Fiber: 8g; Protein: 15g; Sodium: 1,074mg

Cauliflower Mac and Cheese

Serves 6 / **Prep time:** 10 minutes / **Cook time:** 20 minutes

Sometimes we just crave the foods of our childhood. This recipe for vegetarian mac and cheese is reminiscent of the boxed stuff you may have grown up on. Normally, I would encourage swapping out the standard pasta for a protein-rich chickpea or lentil pasta, but in this case, since you'll be cooking the noodles in one pan with the rest of the ingredients, I recommend using classic pasta; legume pasta needs to be drained and rinsed.

1½ cups fresh cauliflower florets

1 cup whole walnuts

2 tablespoons
extra-virgin olive oil

1 tablespoon cornstarch

1 tablespoon paprika

1½ teaspoons garlic powder

1½ teaspoons onion powder

1½ teaspoons sea salt

½ teaspoon freshly ground
black pepper

2 cups water

1½ cups milk of choice

2 cups medium shell noodles

2 cups shredded
Cheddar cheese

1. Put the cauliflower and walnuts in a high-powered blender or food processor. Pulse continually until the texture resembles ground meat.

2. In a large skillet with a lid, heat the oil over medium-high heat.

3. Add the cauliflower-walnut mixture and sauté for about 4 minutes, or until the mixture begins to brown.

4. Sprinkle the cornstarch, paprika, garlic powder, onion powder, salt, and pepper over the cauliflower. Stir to evenly distribute the spices.

5. Add the water, milk, and noodles. Bring to a boil.

6. Cover the skillet with the lid and reduce the heat to a simmer. Cook for 8 to 11 minutes, or until the noodles are al dente.

7. Add the cheese and stir until melted. Remove from the heat. Let stand for a few minutes, or until the sauce thickens a bit. Serve hot.

Tip: You could replace the cauliflower and walnuts with 1 pound of vegan ground meat, like Beyond Meat.

Per Serving: Calories: 488; Total fat: 31g; Carbohydrates: 36g; Fiber: 3g; Protein: 19g; Sodium: 863mg

**Pickled Red Onions,
page 144**

CHAPTER 7

Homemade Staples

Vegetarian Bacon

● **VEGAN**

Serves 6 / **Prep time:** 5 minutes / **Cook time:** 15 minutes

Although nothing will perfectly replace the taste and texture of bacon, don't let that stop you from falling in love with these crispy, smoky morsels. Not only are they fabulous as a snack, but also they are great for VLT Sandwiches (page 88) and pretty much any salad you can dream up. You can even use them to top soups like Pumpkin and White Bean Chili (page 70). You'll be surprised by just how much they mimic the real thing.

1¼ cups large unsweetened coconut flakes

1 tablespoon avocado oil

2 teaspoons soy sauce

1½ teaspoons liquid smoke

1 teaspoon smoked paprika

Pinch salt

Pinch freshly ground black pepper

1. Preheat the oven to 325°F. Line a rimmed sheet pan with parchment paper.

2. In a large bowl, combine the coconut flakes, oil, soy sauce, liquid smoke, and paprika. Season with the salt and pepper. Toss to coat.

3. Spread the mixture out in a single layer on the prepared sheet pan.

4. Transfer the sheet pan to the oven and bake for 6 minutes. Toss, then bake for 6 to 8 more minutes, or until the "bacon" is golden brown. (Make sure you watch very closely in the last few minutes to prevent burning.)

● **Tip:** Store the "bacon" in an airtight container at room temperature for up to 1 week.

Per Serving: Calories: 132; Total fat: 13g; Carbohydrates: 4g; Fiber: 3g; Protein: 1g; Sodium: 104mg

Cashew-Basil Pesto

● **GLUTEN-FREE** ● **SUPERFAST**
Makes 1 cup / **Prep time:** 5 minutes

Traditionally, basil pesto is made with pine nuts. In this spin, I use cashews, which add a unique creaminess that sets this pesto apart. Bonus: Cashews tend to be much cheaper than pine nuts. Feel free to swap out the Parmesan for ¼ cup of nutritional yeast to make this recipe vegan. It won't take you long to realize that you need a batch of this in the freezer at all times.

2 cups basil leaves, packed
½ cup extra-virgin olive oil
½ cup shredded
  Parmesan cheese
⅓ cup raw cashews
3 garlic cloves

2 teaspoons freshly squeezed
  lemon juice
½ teaspoon sea salt
⅛ teaspoon freshly ground
  black pepper

Put the basil, oil, cheese, cashews, garlic, lemon juice, salt, and pepper in a high-powered blender or food processor. Pulse a few times, then blend on high speed for about 1 minute, or until you have a creamy pesto.

● **Tip:** My favorite way to store this dish is by filling ice cube trays with pesto and freezing. These little frozen cubes of pesto thaw rather quickly and can be added to hot dishes immediately for ease and convenience. The pesto can be stored in the freezer for up to 6 months.

Per Batch: Calories: 337; Total fat: 34g; Carbohydrates: 9g; Fiber: 1g; Protein: 3g; Sodium: 426mg

Pickled Red Onions

● GLUTEN-FREE ● VEGAN
Makes 1 cup / **Prep time:** 25 minutes / **Cook time:** 5 minutes

Pickled Red Onions are a staple item in my refrigerator. This bright condiment imparts a lively tang to almost everything, along with a splash of color. They take about 30 minutes to make and last for weeks in the refrigerator. Add to sandwiches, tacos, bean dishes, and mayonnaise-based salads like potato or egg salad.

4 cups water

¾ cup rice vinegar, distilled white vinegar, or apple cider vinegar

½ teaspoon raw cane sugar

½ teaspoon sea salt

1 garlic clove, halved

5 black peppercorns

1 small dried chile de árbol or Thai chile

5 allspice berries (optional)

3 small thyme sprigs (optional)

1 medium red onion, thinly sliced

1. In a pot or kettle, bring the water to a boil over high heat. Remove from the heat.

2. In a large glass jar, combine the vinegar, sugar, salt, garlic, peppercorns, chile, allspice (if using), and thyme (if using). Stir to dissolve the sugar and salt.

3. Place the onion in a colander in the sink. Carefully pour the boiling water over it.

4. Add the onion to the jar and stir to combine. Let cool at room temperature.

5. Cover the jar and refrigerate. The onion can be used right away but is better after a few hours.

Per Batch: Calories: 24; Total fat: 0g; Carbohydrates: 4g; Fiber: 1g; Protein: <1g; Sodium: 581

Avocado Ranch Dressing

● **GLUTEN-FREE**   ● **SUPERFAST**
Makes 1 cup / **Prep time:** 10 minutes

I was raised in the '90s, which means I grew up on ranch dressing. It also means I'm an avocado-loving millennial. This Avocado Ranch Dressing is a healthier, grown-up version of the classic favorite. It still has a creamy tang thanks to the Greek yogurt, but it's full of healthy fats and a little added protein. If you're anything like me, you'll enjoy this with everything from crudités to leftover pizza.

1 large ripe avocado, pitted and peeled

¼ cup plain Greek yogurt

2 teaspoons freshly squeezed lemon juice

1 small garlic clove

½ teaspoon dried parsley

½ teaspoon dried dill

½ teaspoon dried chives

½ teaspoon onion powder

¼ teaspoon sea salt

½ cup almond milk

Put the avocado, yogurt, lemon juice, garlic, parsley, dill, chives, onion powder, salt, and almond milk in a high-powered blender or food processor. Blend until smooth. Serve immediately, or store in an airtight container in the refrigerator for up to 3 days.

Per Batch: Calories: 91; Total fat: 9g; Carbohydrates: 4g; Fiber: 2g; Protein: 2g; Sodium: 81mg

Romesco Sauce

● SUPERFAST ● VEGAN
Makes 1½ cups / Prep time: 5 minutes

Flavor bombs like this Romesco Sauce are essential in vegetarian cooking to bring much-needed complexity to a dish. Romesco is a Spanish tomato- and red pepper–based sauce that's traditionally used for topping fish and vegetables. You'll flip for it in Roasted Eggplant Panini with Romesco Sauce (page 100). Trust me when I say you'll come back to this one again and again.

1 large jarred roasted red pepper, coarsely chopped

2 garlic cloves, coarsely chopped

½ cup toasted slivered almonds

½ cup stale baguette, ripped into small pieces or croutons

2 Roma tomatoes, coarsely chopped

2 tablespoons chopped fresh parsley

2 tablespoons red wine vinegar

1 teaspoon smoked paprika

½ teaspoon cayenne pepper

¼ teaspoon sea salt

Pinch freshly ground black pepper

½ cup extra-virgin olive oil

1. Put the roasted red pepper, garlic, almonds, baguette, tomatoes, parsley, vinegar, paprika, cayenne, salt, and black pepper in a high-powered blender or food processor. Pulse until finely chopped.

2. With the motor running, slowly add the oil and process until smooth.

● **Tip:** You can store your Romesco Sauce in an airtight container in the refrigerator for 7 to 10 days.

Per Batch: Calories: 1,418; Total fat: 137g; Carbohydrates: 41g; Fiber: 13g; Protein: 17g; Sodium: 884mg

Green Goddess Hummus

● **GLUTEN-FREE** ● **SUPERFAST** ● **VEGAN**

Makes 2 cups / **Prep time:** 5 minutes

Hummus of any kind is a true workhorse in the vegetarian kitchen. It masquerades as a high-protein snack with veggies and pita chips and as a flavor-packed spread for bowls and sandwiches. This iteration is full of bright herbs to give it a fresh punch and a lovely green color. Try it in my Falafel and Hummus Bowls (page 40) or Garden Vegetable Wraps (page 89).

1 (15-ounce) can chickpeas, drained and rinsed

½ cup tahini

3 tablespoons freshly squeezed lemon juice, plus more if desired

2 large garlic cloves

1 teaspoon sea salt

½ cup chopped fresh parsley

½ cup chopped fresh basil leaves

¼ cup chopped fresh chives

2 tablespoons extra-virgin olive oil

1. Put the chickpeas, tahini, lemon juice, garlic, salt, parsley, basil, and chives in a high-powered blender or food processor. Blend until smooth.

2. With the machine running, drizzle in the oil until the hummus is completely smooth. If you'd like to thin it out, add 1 tablespoon of water at a time until it reaches your desired consistency. Use immediately, or store in an airtight container in the refrigerator for up to 4 days.

● **Tip:** This is a great opportunity to sneak in some extra veggies. Throw in ½ cup of baby spinach while blending and no one will ever know. You may have to add a little more olive oil or water to compensate.

Per Batch: Calories: 326; Total fat: 24g; Carbohydrates: 21g; Fiber: 7g; Protein: 10g; Sodium: 742mg

Crispy Garlic Chickpeas

● GLUTEN-FREE ● VEGAN

Makes 2 cups / **Prep time:** 5 minutes / **Cook time:** 25 minutes

When I meal prep, I like to prepare elements of dishes that I can use throughout the week in different recipes, as well as for snacking. Precut veggies, hard-boiled eggs, and these Crispy Garlic Chickpeas are a few of my favorites to keep on hand. They're not only an amazing crunchy chip alternative, they're perfect in salads, on top of soups, and even tossed into pasta.

1 (15-ounce) can chickpeas, drained and rinsed

1 tablespoon extra-virgin olive oil

¼ teaspoon sea salt

¼ teaspoon freshly ground black pepper

½ teaspoon garlic powder

1. Put a sheet pan in the oven. Preheat the oven to 450°F.

2. Using a clean kitchen towel or paper towels, pat the chickpeas dry. (You don't want any excess moisture that would prevent crisping.)

3. In a bowl, toss together the chickpeas, oil, salt, pepper, and garlic powder.

4. Carefully remove the sheet pan from the oven, pour the chickpeas on, give the pan a shake, and return it to the oven. Roast, shaking the pan halfway through, for 20 to 25 minutes, or until the chickpeas are crispy. Remove from the oven.

Per Batch: Calories: 528; Total fat: 20g; Carbohydrates: 68g; Fiber: 19g; Protein: 22g; Sodium: 329mg

Lemon-Tahini Sauce

● **GLUTEN-FREE** ● **SUPERFAST** ● **VEGAN**
Makes 1 cup / **Prep time:** 5 minutes

Tahini is one of the most popular pantry staples of the last few years. It's a Middle Eastern condiment similar to nut butter because it consists of only sesame seeds blended with oil and salt. I'll often use it alone, but it's amazing when mixed with other ingredients to make a delicious sauce or hummus, which is what it's known for. You'll use it in Chickpea Pita with Lemon-Tahini Sauce (page 102) and likely much more than that from now on.

⅓ **cup tahini**

⅓ **cup water**

¼ **cup freshly squeezed lemon juice**

2 garlic cloves, minced

½ **teaspoon ground cumin**

¼ **teaspoon cayenne pepper**

¼ **teaspoon sea salt**

Put the tahini, water, lemon juice, garlic, cumin, cayenne, and salt in a high-powered blender or food processor. Blend until smooth.

● **Tip:** This sauce can be stored in an airtight container in the refrigerator for up to 7 days.

Per Batch: Calories: 499; Total fat: 43g; Carbohydrates: 24g; Fiber: 8g; Protein: 14g; Sodium: 676mg

Cilantro-Lime Crema

● GLUTEN-FREE ● SUPERFAST
Makes 1¼ cups / **Prep time:** 5 minutes

I'm a known taco and burrito lover. This sauce is featured in the Quick Chilaquiles (page 30), but there are so many dishes that you can drizzle, slather, or dollop this sauce on. It's also easily adaptable. I'll often add a few pickled jalapeños to the blender and eat it with my favorite tortilla chips. As the name suggests, you can also use Mexican crema in place of sour cream if you can find it.

1¼ cups full-fat sour cream

2 tablespoons freshly squeezed lime juice

½ teaspoon grated lime zest

¼ cup chopped fresh cilantro

¼ teaspoon garlic powder

¼ teaspoon honey

¼ teaspoon sea salt

Put the sour cream, lime juice, lime zest, cilantro, garlic powder, honey, and salt in a high-powered blender or food processor. Blend until smooth.

● **Tip:** If you find that your crema is runnier than you'd like, try blending only part of the sour cream and stirring in the rest.

Per Batch: Calories: 571; Total fat: 57g; Carbohydrates: 13g; Fiber: 0g; Protein: 6g; Sodium: 719mg

Pico de Gallo

● **GLUTEN-FREE** ● **SUPERFAST** ● **VEGAN**
Makes 1¼ cups / Prep time: 10 minutes

If I were a betting lady, I would put money on you using this recipe and the one before it together quite often. Pico de Gallo is a fresh chopped salsa that's perfect with chips for predinner snacking, but it's also a great hack for adding flavor to dishes like Bean and Cheese Flautas (page 103). To lower the heat level, make sure to remove the ribs and seeds from your jalapeño to make it less spicy. Feel free to make a batch (or two) to have on hand for any dish you want to add it to; it will keep in the refrigerator for up to 4 days.

4 medium-ripe tomatoes, diced

1 jalapeño, minced

2 tablespoons freshly squeezed
  lime juice

2 garlic cloves, minced

1 teaspoon sea salt

½ cup diced red onion

½ cup chopped fresh cilantro

Pinch freshly ground
  black pepper

In a large bowl, combine the tomatoes, jalapeño, lime juice, garlic, salt, onion, cilantro, and black pepper. Let sit for at least 10 minutes or overnight in the refrigerator.

● **Make It Faster:** There is a fair bit of dicing in this recipe. If you prefer, you can coarsely chop everything and throw it in a high-powered blender or food processor. Pulse until it is still chunky but there are no large pieces of anything left.

Per Batch: Calories: 143; Total fat: 1g; Carbohydrates: 32g; Fiber: 8g; Protein: 6g; Sodium: 2,359mg

MEASUREMENT CONVERSIONS

VOLUME EQUIVALENTS	US STANDARD	US STANDARD (OUNCES)	METRIC (APPROXIMATE)
LIQUID	2 tablespoons	1 fl. oz.	30 mL
	¼ cup	2 fl. oz.	60 mL
	½ cup	4 fl. oz.	120 mL
	1 cup	8 fl. oz.	240 mL
	1½ cups	12 fl. oz.	355 mL
	2 cups or 1 pint	16 fl. oz.	475 mL
	4 cups or 1 quart	32 fl. oz.	1 L
	1 gallon	128 fl. oz.	4 L
DRY	⅛ teaspoon	–	0.5 mL
	¼ teaspoon	–	1 mL
	½ teaspoon	–	2 mL
	¾ teaspoon	–	4 mL
	1 teaspoon	–	5 mL
	1 tablespoon	–	15 mL
	¼ cup	–	59 mL
	⅓ cup	–	79 mL
	½ cup	–	118 mL
	⅔ cup	–	156 mL
	¾ cup	–	177 mL
	1 cup	–	235 mL
	2 cups or 1 pint	–	475 mL
	3 cups	–	700 mL
	4 cups or 1 quart	–	1 L
	½ gallon	–	2 L
	1 gallon	–	4 L

OVEN TEMPERATURES

FAHRENHEIT	CELSIUS (APPROXIMATE)
250°F	120°C
300°F	150°C
325°F	165°C
350°F	180°C
375°F	190°C
400°F	200°C
425°F	220°C
450°F	230°C

WEIGHT EQUIVALENTS

US STANDARD	METRIC (APPROXIMATE)
½ ounce	15 g
1 ounce	30 g
2 ounces	60 g
4 ounces	115 g
8 ounces	225 g
12 ounces	340 g
16 ounces or 1 pound	455 g

RESOURCES

Healthline.com

It's hard to know where to turn when researching the nutritional profile of ingredients, certain micronutrients, vitamins, and minerals without having to dive into Google Scholar. Healthline thoroughly researches all of its articles and fact-checks with medical professionals and experts, which provides readers with a wealth of knowledge.

MayoClinic.org

Deciphering fact from fiction isn't an easy task when it comes to diet culture and health. I always turn to the Mayo Clinic if I want to double-check something I've read online regarding new studies in the plant-based world.

Nutrition.gov

To stay on top of health recommendations as a whole, this website by the US Department of Agriculture is top-notch. Whether you're trying to get more information for your veggie-curious kids or compare different diets, this is a resource you can trust.

The 5-Ingredient Vegetarian Cookbook: 75 Effortless Recipes for Busy Cooks by Paige Rhodes

For more quick and easy vegetarian recipes, check out my previous book! This vegetarian cookbook shows you how to make quick and flavorful meals, with tasty recipes that require just five ingredients and only a few steps to prepare. For full-time vegetarians or home cooks who just want to add more meatless meals to their rotation, this vegetarian cookbook helps build a repertoire of easy, plant-focused, and budget-friendly recipes the whole family will love.

INDEX

Acknowledgments

It almost seems unfair that my name gets to be on the cover of this book when there are so many people who made it possible: to my husband, Matt, who defines selflessness with every sacrifice that he makes for me to succeed in my dreams.

Thank you to each of the team members at Callisto Media who worked on this book. Collaborating with a team that so highly values diversity, inclusivity, and innovation in every way has been an absolute dream.

I can't skip over the loyal readers of my blog, *My Modern Cookery*. Whether you're frequently in contact on social media or you're a silent scroller, my gratitude knows no bounds.

To my daughter, Norah, I thank you most of all. I hope that through my hard work, you see that women can achieve anything they desire, and not even the sky is the limit.

About the Author

Paige Rhodes is the founder of the blog *My Modern Cookery*, a recipe developer, food stylist, content creator, mother, and author of the books *The Home Cook's Guide to Journaling* and *The 5-Ingredient Vegetarian Cookbook*. After showing an interest in both cooking and writing, she attended culinary school at Sullivan University in Louisville, Kentucky, where she built on her lifelong passion for the culinary arts.

She has written for many online and print publications such as Hearst, Food52, *Country Sampler*, the *Voice-Tribune*, and *Today's Woman*. She's been featured in BuzzFeed articles, the Draper James blog, Brit + Co, and many more. Paige has created a large community of home cooks who join her daily in her love for wholesome food, family, and conversation. You can find her blog at MyModernCookery.com or at @mymoderncookery on all social media channels.

CPSIA information can be obtained
at www.ICGtesting.com
Printed in the USA
JSHW011904050522
25428JS00001B/1

9 781638 782100